Historical Wig Styling: Victorian to the Present

THE FOCAL PRESS COSTUME TOPICS SERIES

Costumes are one of the most important aspects of any production. They are essential tools that create a new reality for both the actor and audience member, which is why you want them to look flawless! Luckily, we're here to help with The Focal Press Costume Topics Series; offering books that explain how to design, construct, and accessorize costumes from a variety of genres and time periods. Step-by-step projects ensure you never get lost or lose inspiration for your design. Let us lend you a hand (or a needle or a comb) with your next costume endeavor!

Titles in The Focal Press Costume Topics Series:

Historical Wig Styling: Victorian to the Present

Allison Lowery

Focal Press
Taylor & Francis Group

NEW YORK AND LONDON

First published 2013
by Focal Press
70 Blanchard Rd Suite 402
Burlington, MA 01803

Simultaneously published in the UK
by Focal Press
2 Park Square, Milton Park, Abingdon, Oxon OX14 4RN

Focal Press is an imprint of the Taylor & Francis Group, an Informa business

Notices
Knowledge and best practice in this field are constantly changing. As new research
and experience broaden our understanding, changes in research methods, professional
practices, or medical treatment may become necessary.

Practitioners and researchers must always rely on their own experience and knowledge
in evaluating and using any information, methods, compounds, or experiments
described herein. In using such information or methods they should be mindful of
their own safety and the safety of others, including parties for whom they have a
professional responsibility.

Product or corporate names may be trademarks or registered trademarks, and are used
only for identification and explanation without intent to infringe.

Library of Congress Cataloging in Publication Data

Lowery, Allison.
Historical wig styling. Victorian to the present / Allison Lowery.
pages cm
1. Wigs--Design and construction. 2. Hairdressing. 3. Hairstyles--History. I. Title.
TT975.L832 2013
646.7'248--dc23
2012035378

ISBN: 978-0-240-82124-5 (pbk)
ISBN: 978-0-240-82141-2 (ebk)

Typeset in Adobe Garamond
By TNQ Books and Journals, Chennai, India

Printed by 1010 Printing International Limited

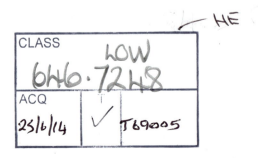

{ contents }

{ *acknowledgments* }

So many people have helped to make this book possible. Many heartfelt thanks go out to the amazing Stacey Walker, Emma Elder and the staff at Focal Press/Taylor and Francis; Kristina Tollefson, technical editor/reader of the highest quality; Texas Performing Arts and the Texas Performing Arts Costume Shop, especially Kathy Panoff and Patricia Risser; the University of Texas Department of Theatre and Dance; Wendy Zieger and the Bridgeman Art Library; Wikipedia Commons; Everything Vintage; my teachers and mentors, Martha Ruskai and Patricia Wesp; the insanely amazing Tim Babiak for the most rocking amazing photography and collaboration anyone could ask for; the models—Emma Dirks, Anna Fugate, Leslie Hethcox, Ariel Livingston, Sabrina Lotfi, Marsherrie Madkins, Josephine McAdam, and Ivy Negron—for being incredible style chameleons; my students—Tara Cooper, Emma Dirks, Anna Fugate, Thumper Gosney, Beauty Kampf-Thibodeau, Josephine McAdam, Kara Meche, Lexi O'Reilly, Bethany Renfro, Maur Sela, Sarah Shade, and Elisa Solomon, for being a constant source of inspiration; Stephanie Williams Caillabet; Amanda French; Darren Jinks; Rick Jarvie; Susan Branch Towne; Dennis and Jeffrey at Elsen Associates; the Friday Night Gamers—Terry, Sheena, Jeff, Sam, Charles, Brad, Chris, and Irving; the TXRD Lonestar Rollergirls (Cherry Bombs destroy!); the TXRD BWs, especially Pinto, Sheryl, Chicago Jimmy, Sword, Amy, and Mama Peno; Jim's Restaurant; Dave and Patti; *Cher* Uncle, Arthur Hall Smith, for helping to give me my love of art; my brother, Scott; my grandparents, Jack and Elizabeth Karnes (Grandma, you will always be my favorite 1940s redhead–RIP); Mom (thank you for the never ending love and encouragement) and Dad (how I wish you could have seen this finished); and especially to Terry, without whose love and support this book would not have been finished.

—Allison Lowery

one

INTRODUCTION TO WIG STYLING TECHNIQUES

Figure 1.1 Wig styling student Maur Sela works on styling a lace front wig.

Welcome to the wonderful and sometime mysterious world of wig styling! Wigs can be a great asset to any theatrical costume or historical costume recreation. Learning the techniques of wig styling can help everyone achieve the completely authentic look they are striving for. Wigs give you the ability to create many looks that would take a long time to create with someone's real hair—wigs have the advantage of being able to be prepped ahead of time so that they are ready to put on at a moment's notice, which saves valuable time with your performer! This is especially helpful if you are working on a theatrical production and you only have an hour and a half to get a cast of twenty people ready in historical looks. The techniques presented in this book will help you create a wide number of different hairstyles from different eras of history. Many of these techniques can also be adapted for use on someone's real hair if a wig or hairpiece is not an option. I hope this book will be used by theatre technicians, film technicians, historical re-enactors, fashion professionals, hairstylists, cosplayers, and anyone else looking to create unique and elaborate hairstyles.

Tools, Supplies, and Hair Products

There are a number of tools and products you need to assemble before you begin your journey into wig styling. For suggestions about where to find these items, please refer to Appendix 3 at the back of the book. Here is a list of things you will need:

1. Wigs! All kinds! I most often use lace front wigs that have had their front hairline knotted by hand onto fine lace. While I prefer lace front wigs (their realistic look creates the most authentic looking hairstyles), hard front wigs (wigs that are the easiest to find commercially) can be used to great effect as well. I use equal numbers of human hair wigs and synthetic wigs. I prefer human hair wigs for men's wigs, long loose-hanging wigs (human hair has weight that allows it to hang more naturally than synthetic hair), and for situations where there may only be one or two wigs in a production. Synthetic fiber holds its curl better, which makes it ideal for long running shows, outdoor theatre, or shows where there is vigorous physical activity such as dancing or fighting. Human hair wigs are styled by a combination of wetness, heat, and styling products; synthetic wigs are set using steam.

2. A wig block (also sometimes called the head block). A wig block is a canvas head that is made for styling and making wigs. It is made of canvas and filled with sawdust so that the block is sturdy and easy to pin into. Wig blocks are available in a range of head

sizes. It is important to note that Styrofoam heads are not the same as a wig block. Styrofoam heads are best used for storing a wig that has already been styled. Styrofoam shrinks (sometimes extremely) when heat is applied to it. Therefore, attempting to style a wig with heat (either with steam or by putting the head in a warm wig dryer) can cause the Styrofoam head to distort, making it very difficult to continue styling the wig.

Figure 1.2 A lace front wig on a canvas wig block that is being held onto the table by a wig clamp.

3. A wig clamp. This is a clamp that attaches to the edge of a table so that you may work on your wig without worrying about it falling off of the table. Wig clamps come in both metal and plastic—both work well.

4. Blocking tape. These are pieces of fabric or ribbon that hold the edge of a lace front wig flat while you are working. I prefer to use bias tape or twill tape. Ribbons or shoelaces will also work as blocking tape.

These tapes are also sometimes used to hold a style in place as you work to create waves. Blocking tape can be used over and over again.

5. Pins. You will need two kinds of pins. Blocking pins are the pins you will use to secure the wig to the head block. I prefer to use quilter's pins with round heads, but corsage pins can also be used. These are easy to remove from the block when needed, and their round heads do not snag in the hair when you are styling the wig. You will also need t-pins. These are t-shaped pins that are used to secure rollers to the head. For both blocking pins and t-pins, the longest length you can find is ideal.

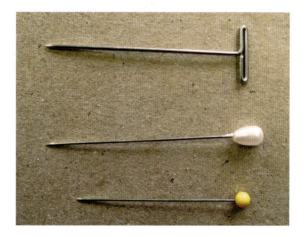

Figure 1.3 From top: a t-pin, a corsage pin, and a round head pin.

6. Rollers. You will need a variety of sizes of rollers. The largest size I use is 1¾ inch diameter rollers. All sizes smaller than that are the most useful. The three sizes I use most often are nickel-sized (7/8 inch diameter), dime-sized (5/8 inch diameter), and pencil-sized (3/8 inch diameter). I use both wire rollers (sometimes called spring wire rollers) and plastic rollers. Wire rollers are easier to pin into when you

are working; otherwise, I have not noticed much difference between them. Note that wire rollers usually come with a bristle brush inside them. I always remove this little brush before using the rollers. I also like to use perm rods for tiny curls.

Figure 1.4   This is a good sample assortment of roller types and sizes.

7. End wraps, also known as end papers. These are used to smooth the ends of the hair so they wrap neatly around the end of the roller. End papers are sold by the box. One box should last you through at least 15 hairstyles.

8. A spray bottle. You will fill the spray bottle with water so that you can wet the wig as you work. Large or small size spray bottles are fine—I prefer large so that I do not have to refill it as often. Other people are more comfortable using a smaller bottle.

9. Combs and brushes. You will also need a variety of combs and brushes to set and style the wig. I consider the following brushes essential:

   • A wide toothed comb. This is used for detangling wet wigs and for combing through hair when a brush would disturb the curl too much.

   • A rat tail comb. These are used for sectioning the hair, making clean parts, and for removing all tangles from the hair.

   • A teasing/smoothing brush. This brush is absolutely essential. It is used for teasing or back-combing the hair, smoothing curls around your finger, controlling flyaway messy hairs, and many other things.

   • A teasing/lifting comb. This comb is not only used to tease hair, but also to lift or "pick out" a voluminous hairstyle so that it is even larger.

   • A large wire brush, often called a cushion brush. This brush is used for brushing through the entire wig once you have removed the rollers. I often use dog brushes for this. I also prefer brushes that do not have tipped bristles. I have found that the tips eventually come off and I end up spending time picking the tips out of the wig.

Figure 1.5   From left to right: a wide-toothed comb, a rat tail comb, a teasing/smoothing brush, a teasing/lifting comb, and a large wire brush.

10. Styling clips. You will need an assortment of small, pronged curl clips (available in both single and double pronged style); long clips that are called either duckbill clips or alligator clips; and butterfly clips. The clips are used to hold sections of hair in place and for pin curl setting.

Figure 1.6 From left: butterfly clips, a single-prong curl clip, a double-prong curl clip, and a variety of duckbill/alligator clips.

11. Hair styling pins. You will need a variety of pins once you get to the point of combing out and styling your wig. Black and brown bobby pins, black and bronze hairpins, and three inch hairpins (often referred to as "wig pins") are all necessary. Silver pins can also be useful when you are working with white or grey wigs. It is a good idea to match the color of the pin to the color of the wig you are styling.

12. A wig dryer. Once the wig has been set, it will need to be dried in a wig dryer. There are commercially available wig dryers available for purchase (Figure 1.8).

You can also make your own (Figure 1.9) by putting a hair dryer in a hole cut into a large box (either cardboard or wooden—wood is preferred). An important note: if you do make your own wig dryer, you must keep an eye on it while the hair dryer is on! You do not want the hair dryer to overheat and start a fire. It is also important to make sure that the hair dryer is far enough away from the wig so that the heat from the dryer does not scorch or melt the hair. Angle the hair dryer so that it is not blowing directly on the wig.

13. A small hand steamer. When you are setting a synthetic wig, the curl must be set with steam. A small hand steamer makes it easy to control the direction of the steam and to ensure that every roller is attended to. There are also commercial wig steamers available on the market, but I prefer the smaller hand steamers because they afford more control. Full size steamers and hat steamers also work in a pinch.

Figure 1.7 From the top: a three-inch wig pin, a hair pin, and a bobby pin.

Figure 1.8 A commercial wig dryer.

Figure 1.9 A "homemade" wig dryer, using a cardboard box and a commercial hair dryer. The box flaps have been folded in so that the placement of the dryer and the placement of the head block are visible. When you are drying a wig, these flaps should be folded so that the box is closed.

Figuer 1.10 A small hand-held steamer being used to steam a synthetic wig.

14. Hairnets, rubber bands/hair elastics, and rats. Hairnets in a variety of colors will enable you to create long-lasting, neat-looking hairstyles. Rubber bands and/or hair elastics allow you to secure sections of hair and make ponytails and braids. Rats (hair pads) allow you to add fullness to a wig or hairstyle without having to rely on teasing. Rats can be purchased ready made, or can be created by adding loose hair inside a hairnet and rolling it up into the desired size and shape.

Figure 1.11 An assortment of hairnets, wig rats/pads, and hair elastics.

15. Styling products. I use three different kinds of hair styling products.

    • Hairspray. I prefer aerosol hairspray (as opposed to pump). Whatever brand you prefer is fine.

    • Setting lotion. This lotion is available at beauty supply stores and is used to hold curl and add volume when it is applied to hair as it is being set.

    • Gel. I use the cheapest readily available brand. Gel can also be used as a setting lotion in a pinch. It is also used for slicking down part of a hairstyle.

In general, I avoid styling products that are waxes or pomades. These tend to weight wigs down and make them look clumpy. This can be helpful when you are creating a wig for an unsavory character, but it is more often a hindrance.

16. Hair accessories. Any number of decorative combs, bows, jewelry, flowers, feathers, and other craft supplies can be used to make hair ornaments.

Figure 1.12 An assortment of hair accessories.

17. An apron for covering your clothes. I always wear an apron to help keep hair, water, and styling products off of my clothes.

18. A selection of hairpieces. Hairpieces can be added into wigs that do not have enough hair to create a given style. A variety of colors and sizes of hairpieces is best—wiglets (small, rounded hairpieces), switches (ponytails of hair), and falls (large hairpieces that cover three-quarters of the head) are especially useful.

Figure 1.13 Useful hairpieces, from left: a fall, a switch, and a wiglet.

Figure 1.15 A selection of plastic and wooden dowel rods. The yellow rod is a piece of cut-off broom handle—the tapered end helps it to work especially well.

19. Wefting. Wefting is woven strips of hair used to make wigs, hairpieces, and extensions. Weft can be sewn into wigs to add length or fullness in specific areas.

21. A space to work in. Ideally this space will be well ventilated, well lit, and have a good-sized table for your supplies. You can organize your supplies as best suits you. Some people like shelves, some like cabinets, some like rolling carts.

Figure 1.14 Samples of wefting.

20. A selection of wooden or plastic dowel rods, in similar diameter to the rollers you assembled. Dowel rods can be used for pin curl setting, or for helping to shape finished ringlets and curls.

Figure 1.16 University of Texas students Emma Dirks, Bethany Renfro, Lexi O'Reilly, Sarah Thornell, and Lola Hylton at work in the wig room.

Handling Wigs

Once you have assembled all of your supplies and have done your research so that you know all about the style you want to create, you will be ready to begin styling. But where do you start? First, you must learn some basic points about handling wigs.

Human Hair vs Synthetic Hair

The two main materials that the wigs you will be using are made of are human hair and synthetic hair. (Yak wigs are also sometimes used; follow the same rules for handling them as you would for human hair wigs.)

Human hair wigs are made of the hair from, yes, humans. Human hair wigs are set by getting them very wet and then drying them with heat. Hot tools, such as curling irons, flat irons, and crimping irons may be used on human hair wigs. Human hair wigs move more like a real head of hair. Their sheen is more like that of a real head of hair. They are, however, susceptible to bad hair days just like a real person. Human hair wigs are good choices for short men's wigs, long women's wigs that need to look very natural, and wigs that need to last for a long time.

Synthetic wigs are made of plastic hair that is extruded through a machine. Because of this, synthetic hair can be made in any number of lengths and colors. *Synthetic wigs must always be styled with steam!* This includes any kind of curling, waving, or straightening. *No hot tools must ever touch synthetic wigs!* Flat irons, curling irons, and other hot tools will cause the plastic hair of the wig to melt, which will make it useless. Once the hair has been fried, there is nothing you can do to bring it back. All you can do is cut the fried hair out of the wig and replace it with new hair. There are new types of synthetic hair being developed that can withstand styling with hot tools, but unless the wig instructions explicitly say that it can be styled with

heat, you should assume that you cannot do this. Better safe than sorry! Synthetic wigs are a good choice for when you need unusual colors or excessive length. They are also good for a hairstyle that needs to last—this makes them an excellent choice for vigorous musicals or outdoor theatre. Synthetic wigs hold their style very well. They are also significantly cheaper than human hair wigs.

Hard Front Wigs vs Lace Front Wigs

Both synthetic and human hair wigs will come with one of two kinds of front: a hard front or a lace front. A hard front wig is the most common front for the wig to have. This wig has a bound-off fabric edge that finishes off the entire front part of the wig. This often looks artificial and hard, which is why it is called a hard front. If you are using a hard front wig, you will need to do some tricks to soften the hairstyle around the face so that it looks more natural on the performer. Lace front wigs are wigs that have had the hard front of the wig cut off. The front edge of the wig then has a piece of almost invisible fine lace, known as wig lace, sewn to the front of the wig. Individual hairs are then knotted into this wig lace with a hook, creating the illusion of hair that is growing directly out of the wearer's skin. These wigs look much more realistic. They are also more delicate and must be handled carefully… you should never hold a lace front wig by the lace! A lace front wig can also be a wig that has been made completely from scratch, with all of the hair in the wig being knotted into the lace. These wigs are very lightweight and very natural looking; they are also the most delicate of all the wigs.

Blocking the Wig

Blocking a wig is the act of securing a wig to a wig block with pins before you begin the styling process. Both hard front and lace front wigs must be blocked before you begin working on them. You should never work on a wig that is not properly secured to a wig block—this will cause the wig to slip around on the block or get stretched out of place—possibly even torn.

To block a hard front wig (see Figures 1.17–19):

1. Place the wig block on a wig clamp that is secured to the table.

2. Place the wig on the block. Be sure it is in the proper place on the head—not too far forward or too far back. Check to make sure the side tabs are even.

3. Place a blocking pin in the center front, at each ear tab, and at either side of the nape of the neck. All of these pins should be about one-eighth of an inch from the front of the wig. It is also helpful to place the pins in at a slight angle so that they are less likely to slip out of the wig while you are working.

To block a lace front wig (see Figures 1.20–24):

1. Place the wig block on a wig clamp that is secured to a table.

2. Place the wig on the block, again making sure it is in the right place. Check to make sure that the sides of the hairline are even.

3. Place a blocking pin at either side of the head above each ear, and at either side of the nape of the neck.

4. Use a piece of blocking tape to smooth and hold the lace front in place. The tape should be placed just above the edge of the wig lace. Begin at the center front of the wig and place a blocking pin in the blocking tape. Continue pinning along the hairline, placing a blocking pin every inch or so. Be sure to pin around the hair at the sideburns as well.

5. Secure any loose blocking tape you may have out of the way. This will keep it from getting caught by combs or brushes while you are working.

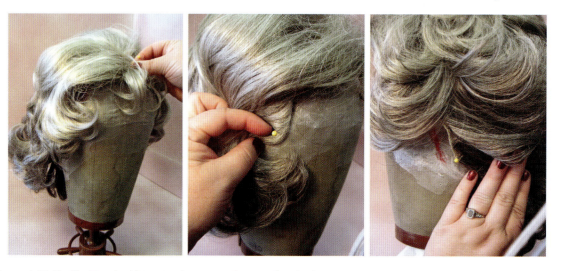

Figures 1.17–19   Blocking a hard front wig: place a pin at the center front hairline (Figure 1.17); at each ear tab (Figure 1.18); and at either side of the nape of the neck (Figure 1.19).

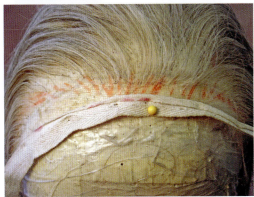

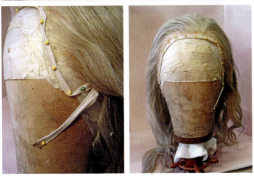

Figures 1.20–24 Blocking a lace front wig. Notice the placement of the blocking pins. Also notice how the tape is secured around the sideburn area (Figure 1.23).

Basic Styling Techniques

Hairstyles are made up of four elements: straight hair, wavy hair, curly hair, and braids/coils/buns. There are a number of ways these different textures can be achieved.

Straight Hair

A human hair wig can be thoroughly wet, combed through and dried to become straight (unless you are working with naturally curly or permed hair). Human hair can also be ironed with a flat iron. To do this, section the hair on the wig into five sections. Begin at the nape of the neck, and run the flat iron through the hair from root to tip. Move from the nape of the neck gradually up to the front hairline of the wig. Work in small sections to get the hair thoroughly straight.

A synthetic wig that is not already straight is straightened by steam. Again, section the wig hair into five sections (the hair should be damp for this). Begin at the nape of the neck. Use a rat tail comb to pull a small section of hair taut. Direct the nozzle of the steamer toward the section of hair at the roots (see Figure 1.25). You should be able to see the hair shaft straighten itself out under the steam. Pull the comb through the hair, moving the steamer along with it until you reach the ends of the hair. Repeat this for every section of the hair, working your way up from the nape of the neck to the front of the hairline. Once the wig is straight, place it in a wig dryer to dry, or allow it to air dry on a shelf.

Figure 1.25 Thumper Gosney demonstrates how to properly steam a synthetic wig.

Figure 1.26 Step.1. Thoroughly saturate the hair with setting lotion. Comb the setting lotion through the hair to make sure it gets all the way to the ends.

Wavy Hair

Wavy hair is hair that ripples in an "S" shape. There are three main methods to achieve wavy hair: water waving (also known as finger waving); pin curling; and roller setting. The kind of waves and how much volume you wish for the end product to have will determine which method of waving you choose. All three methods of waving will be demonstrated on one wig.

Water Waving

Water waving, or finger waving, creates a wave that is extremely flat to the head. When combed out, these waves will be larger and softer than those created by the other waving methods. To create water waves:

Figure 1.27 Step 2. Place the part in the wig wherever you wish for it to be. Comb the hair by the part in one direction (either toward or away from the hairline).

Figure 1.28   Step 3. Once you have the hair combed in the direction you want, secure it by pinning a long piece of blocking tape down the center of the wave. The blocking tape will hold the waves in place as you work.

Figure 1.29   Step 4. To create a more defined ridge in the wave, push up with the ribbon before you pin it down.

Figure 1.30   Step 5. The first half of the wave is pinned in place. Pin the ribbon all along the wave.

Figure 1.31   Step 6. Next, comb the length of the hair in the opposite direction from the direction you started with.

Figure 1.32   Step 7. Use the blocking tape to secure the center of this part of the wave. The first "S" of the wave has been formed.

Figure 1.33   Step 8. Continue working your way down the head, alternating directions. You may need to continue to re-wet the hair as you work—it is important that the hair is thoroughly saturated as you are shaping the waves. You can do waves that go all the way around the head, or you can wave a small section of the hair—it all depends on the style you want!

Figure 1.34   Step 9. For a nice finish at the bottom of a water wave, I will often arrange the hair into a pin curl.

Figure 1.35   Step 10. Dry the wig in the wig dryer for at least 75 minutes. When you are ready to comb out the wig, begin by removing the tape. You should start removing the tape at the top of the wig, not the bottom.

Figure 1.36   Step 11. For a slicker, more shellacked look, you can leave the wig as it is, without combing through the hair.

Figure 1.37   Step 12. If you decide to comb out the waves, begin at the end of the hair and work your way up.

Figure 1.38   Step 13. The combed out wave will be very soft.

Figure 1.39   Step 14. Use duckbill clips to add more definition to the waves, if desired.

Figure 1.40   Step 15. If you wish to neaten the ends of the hair, use a rat tail comb to smooth the ends around your finger.

Once you have completed arranging the waves, mist the wig with hairspray and let it sit overnight. Remove the duckbill clips and the wig should be ready to be worn.

Pin Curling

Pin curling is the traditional method of hair setting that was so popular in the 1930s, 40s, and 50s.

Figure 1.41   Step 1. Again, begin by saturating the hair with setting lotion and combing all of the hair in one direction, starting at the part.

Figure 1.42   Step 2. Use your rat tail comb to separate out a square section of hair, about one inch by one inch.

Figure 1.43   Step 3. Use a dowel rod or other kind of stick to shape your curl and keep it perfectly round. Place an end paper over the ends of the hair, and begin rolling the hair at the tip.

Figure 1.44   Step 4. Once you have wound the hair all the way up to the roots, slide the stick out and secure the curl with pins or clips. (I prefer pins because they do not leave as much of a crimp in the hair.)

Figure 1.45 Step 5. To achieve a perfect wave, the next curls in the row (working down the head from the crown) should go in the same direction. Both of these curls have been wound counter-clockwise.

Figure 1.46 Step 6. When you are ready to do the next row, comb all of the hair in the opposite direction from the first row. (In this example, the first row had the hair combed away from the face, so the second row will be combed toward the face.)

Figure 1.47 Step 7. The next row of pin curls should be wound in the opposite direction as the row above. In this case, the first row was curled counter-clockwise, so the second row is wound clockwise. The arrows indicate the direction.

Figure 1.48 Step 8. Continue setting the second row with the pin curls going clockwise. Again, you may need to re-wet the hair as you are working.

Figure 1.49   Step 9. As you work your way down the head, the curl direction will continue to alternate between counter-clockwise and clockwise. When you are done setting the wig, dry it in the wig dryer for at least 75 minutes.

Figure 1.50   Step 10. To comb out the pin curl set, begin by removing the pin curls from the bottom up.

Figure 1.51   Step 11. Use a rat tail comb to comb through all of the curls.

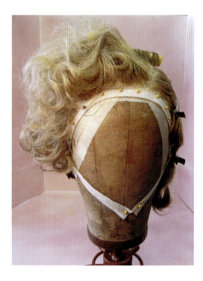

Figure 1.52   Step 12. Notice how much more voluminous the pin curl set is compared to the water wave set.

Figure 1.53 Step 13. Begin pinching the waves with your fingers and pushing the hair round until the waves start to fall into place.

Figure 1.54 Step 14. Use a smoothing brush to flatten down the hair and push the waves into place.

Figure 1.55 Step 15. Pin bias tape in the center of the curve of each section of the wave to set it in place.

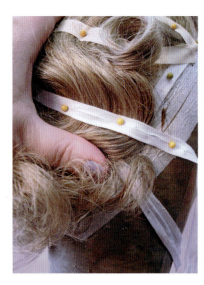

Figure 1.56 Step 16. Use the bias tape and your fingers to push up on the wave to make the ridges more defined.

Figure 1.57   Step 17. When you reach the ends of the hair, use the rat tail comb or the smoothing brush to smooth the curls around your fingers. This will create a clean, neat curl.

Figure 1.58   Step 18. Slide the finished curl off your finger and arrange it in an attractive way.

Just like with the water wave set, when you are finished arranging the curls you should mist the wig with hairspray and let it sit overnight. Remove the bias tape when you are ready for the wig to be worn.

Roller Setting

Using rollers to set the hair is the most effective way to get a round, neat curl. If you push the curl flat, it becomes a wave. A few notes about roller setting:

Figure 1.59   The section of hair is slightly less wide and deep than the plastic roller.

Figure 1.60   The section of hair should be held taut.

1. The section of hair that you are going to set on the roller should never be wider or deeper than the roller itself.

2. When you are rolling a section of hair, be sure to maintain tension on the hair in order to get a nice smooth set. Letting the hair go slack while the wig is being set will result in a messy wig.

Figures 1.61–63   3. A roller can be set on base (Figure 1.61), forward of base (Figure 1.62), or off base with drag (Figure 1.63). Under most circumstances, you will want to set with the roller on base. For a pompadour effect that adds lots of volume, set the roller forward of base. For a flatter look that sits closer to the head, you may need to set the wig off base with drag.

4. Use a t-pin to secure each roller in place. Turn the t-pin so that it is parallel to the hair in the roller. This will help you avoid snagging hair in the t-pin.

Figures 1.64–66   5. Using an endpaper will give your curls much less frizzy ends. To use an endpaper, slip it behind the section of hair (Figure 1.64), fold each side of the endpaper over toward the center (Figure 1.65), spritz the endpaper with water, and slide it down until the ends of the hair are encased (Figure 1.66). You are new ready to proceed with rolling the section of hair onto a roller.

Roller Setting for Waves

Figure 1.67   Step 1. Begin setting the rollers at the part of the wig. These rollers are to be set off base with a small amount of drag. As you work your way down, make sure that the roller in one row sits over where two rows come together in the next row down. This is called a brick set, because the rollers are offset like bricks in a wall.

Figure 1.68   Step 2. Set the wig from top to bottom.

Figure 1.69   Step 3. Steam the wig if it is synthetic hair and put it in the wig dryer for at least 75 minutes. When you are ready to comb out the set, begin removing the rollers from the bottom.

Figure 1.70   Step 4. After you have removed all of the rollers, you will see gaps in the hair. These are called roller breaks.

Figure 1.71   Step 5. Use a wide-toothed comb to gently pick through all of the curls. This will help get rid of the roller breaks.

Figure 1.72　Step 6. Run a smoothing brush through the curls to begin shaping the hair into waves.

Figure 1.73　Step 7. Use your fingers to begin pinching and pushing the waves into shape.

Figure 1.74　Step 8. Use a rat tail comb to push the waves in place. Secure them with bias tape.

Figure 1.75　Step 9. Comb the ends of the curls around your fingers to make them smooth and neat.

When you are done, mist the wig with hairspray and let it sit overnight. Remove the bias tape when you are ready for the wig to be worn.

Figures 1.76–78   One wig, set three ways: a water wave set (Figure 1.76), a pin curl set (Figure 1.77), and a roller set (Figure 1.78).

Curly Hair

Just as there are different sizes and shapes of waved hair, there are also different kinds of curly hair. I will now discuss a variety of methods for creating curly hair.

Roller Setting

Hair can be made curly by setting it on rollers, using the same technique as described in the wavy hair section above. The comb out is different, however. Instead of pressing the hair flat into waves, you need to work with the hair in a looser way.

Figure 1.79   Step 1. Unroll the rollers straight out horizontally.

Figure 1.80   Step 2. If you do not brush the curls out, they will be loose and somewhat clumped together.

Figure 1.81   Step 3. Use a large wooden brush to smooth out the curls and get rid of the clumps.

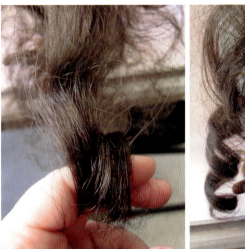

Figure 1.82 Step 4. After brushing, the curls become loose and soft.

Figures 1.83 and 1.84 Step 5. If you want more defined curls, you can brush the ends around your fingers.

Sausage Curls/Ringlets

Sausage curls, or ringlets, are those curls that form a smooth tube of hair. Ideally, there are no gaps in the column of hair. This is a rigid kind of hairstyle that was especially popular in parts of the nineteenth century.

Figure 1.85 Step 1. Separate out a small vertical section of hair and thoroughly wet it.

Figure 1.86 Step 2. Begin rolling the hair around the bottom of the roller.

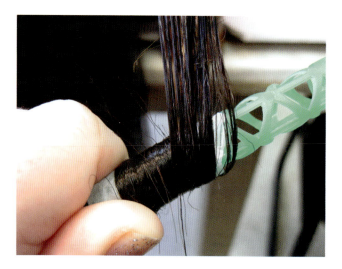

Figure 1.87   Step 3. As you wind the hair around the roller, make sure you overlap some of the hair every time the hair goes around the roller.

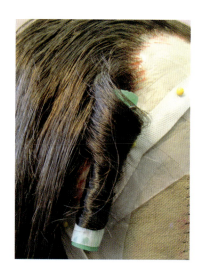

Figure 1.88   Step 4. Pin the roller vertically. Once you have set all of your curls, steam the hair if it is synthetic and dry it in the wig dryer for at least 75 minutes.

Figure 1.89   Step 5. After the hair is dry, unwind it from the roller.

Figure 1.90   Step 6. You will have a column of hair at this point, but it is usually not as neat and tidy as it could be.

Figure 1.91 and 1.92   Step 7. Use an appropriate size of dowel rod and shape the curl by brushing it around the rod.

Figure 1.93   Step 8. Gently slide the dowel rod out of the bottom of the ringlet. You will be left with a smoother, neater sausage curl.

Spiral Curls

Spiral curls are more a combination of a wave and a curl. This is a very natural-looking curl that is useful for styling many historical looks.

Figure 1.94   Step 1. Again, separate out a vertical section of hair. This section of hair should be of fairly substantial thickness. The size of the section will depend a little on how dense the hair is in your wig, but a section that is at least one inch wide by two inches high is a good starting point. If you make this curl with a section of hair that is too thin, you will end up with a lot of tangled frizz.

Figure 1.95   Step 2. Twist the hair in the direction you want the roller to face. Twist the section of hair tightly, but not so tightly that the hair begins to twist back up on itself.

Figure 1.96   Step 3. Begin rolling the twisted section onto the roller at the bottom.

Figure 1.97   Step 4. As you wind the hair up on the roller, the twisted coils should stack up on top of each other.

Figure 1.98   Step 5. When you reach the top, pin the roller vertically. Steam the hair if necessary and dry it in the wig dryer for 75 minutes.

Figure 1.99   Step 6. Once the hair is dry, unwind it from the roller.

Figure 1.101   Step 8. Use your fingers to comb through each section of hair. Each time you comb through the hair, the curls will get softer and less defined. You can also use a wide-toothed comb to comb through the curl.

Figure 1.100   Step 7. Notice the snaky look of the hair as it comes off the roller.

Figure 1.102   Step 9. The finished curl will be very soft and natural looking.

Curl Clusters

Sometimes, you will discover that you need a cluster of curls in a hairstyle.

Figure 1.103   Step 1. Firmly secure the base of the section where you want it by interlocking two bobby pins. This is done by crossing two bobby pins in an "X" shape. Also make sure that you pin into the base of the wig and not just into the hair itself for a really firm hold.

Figure 1.104   Step 2. Brush the hair around your finger with a smoothing brush.

Figure 1.105   Step 3. Loosely bring the bottom of the curl up toward the base and drape it until it looks pretty.

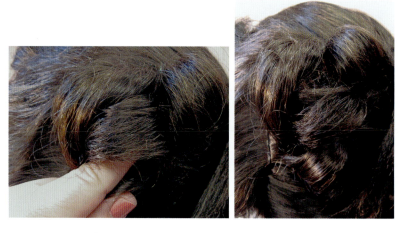

Figures 1.106 and 1.107 Step 4. Secure the arrangement with a couple of bobby pins.

Being able to hide your bobby pins as you work is an important skill. When you are pinning a curl, always place your pins on the inside of a curl (Figure 1.108). When you are pinning a twisted section of hair, insert the pin on the outside of the twist with the bobby pin pointing up (Figure 1.109). Twist the bobby pin up and around into the twist, locking the pin in the inside of the twist (Figure 1.110). Hiding your pins is important whether you are using bobby pins, hair pins, or wig pins. It is also important not to try to pin too much hair at once. If your pin wants to slide back out of a section of hair, it probably means that you are attempting to put too much hair in your pin.

Figures 1.108–110 From left: Figure 1.108—Hiding a bobby pin inside a curl; Figures 1.109 and 1.110—Hiding your bobby pin inside a twist.

Braided Hair

Another commonly used style element is the braid. Braids are a simple, quick way to create a period look.

Traditional Braid

Figure 1.111   Step 1. Separate the section of hair into three strands.

Figure 1.112   Step 2. Cross one of the outside sections over the middle section so that it becomes the new middle section.

Figure 1.113   Step 3. Cross the other outside section over into the middle.

Figures 1.114 and 1.115   Step 4. Repeat this process until you reach the ends of the hair. Secure the end of the braid with a rubber band or elastic that matches the hair color.

French Braid/Reverse French Braid

A French braid is a braid where not all of the hair is braided at once, and pieces of hair are added into the three sections as you make the braid. This results in a braid that sits very flat to the head and does not create a lot of bulk.

Figure 1.116 Step 1. Separate the hair into three small sections at the top of where you want the braid to begin. The size of the sections will be determined by how intricate you wish the braid to look.

Figure 1.117 Step 2. Braid the hair the same way you did for the traditional braid, crossing the outside sections over to the middle section.

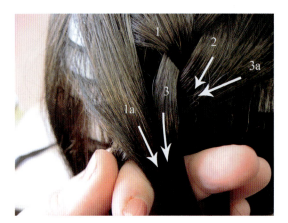

Figure 1.118 Step 3. After making the initial pass through the original hair sections, begin adding more hair to the braid by picking up small sections of hair to add in as you work.

Figure 1.119 Step 4. Continue working your way down the braid, adding sections as you go. The finished braid will sit neatly against the head.

In a reverse French braid (sometimes called a Dutch braid), instead of crossing the section over to the center, you will instead cross them underneath to the center. This will cause the finished braid to look like it is sitting on top of the hair, but still allows the braid to sit very close to the head.

Figure 1.120   Step 1. Again, begin by dividing the hair into three sections.

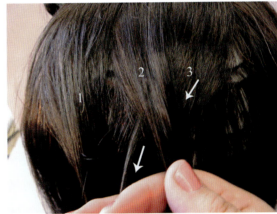

Figure 1.121   Step 2. Cross the outside section under the middle section to begin the braid.

Figure 1.122   Step 3. After you make the initial pass through the first three sections of hair, begin picking up small sections of hair to add into the braid.

Figure 1.123   Step 4. Keep adding sections of hair to the braid until you run out of hair, continuing to cross the sections underneath as you work. Secure the end of the braid with an elastic band. The finished braid will look as though it is sitting on top of the hair.

Rope Braid

A rope braid is a two-strand braid where the sections are twisted together. It is an especially nice braid to use in period hairstyles.

Figure 1.124   Step 1. Separate the hair into two sections. You can either begin with the hair in a ponytail, or with two loose sections of hair.

Figure 1.125   Step 2. Twist each section of hair in the same direction. For example, if you twist one section to the right, you must also twist the second section to the right. Do not twist the sections so tightly that they begin to twist back up on themselves.

Figure 1.126   Step 3. Twist the coiled sections of hair together in the opposite direction from the one you did the initial twisting in. For example, if you twisted each section to the right in step 2, you would then twist the two sections together to the left. Secure the end of the braid with an elastic band.

Figure 1.127   Step 4. The finished rope braid.

Fishtail/Herringbone Braid

The fishtail (or herringbone) braid is another braid that begins with two sections of hair. It is another nice braid to use in period hairstyling.

Figure 1.128   Step 1. Divide the hair into two sections. Again, you either start with the hair already in a ponytail, or with two sections of loose hair.

Figure 1.129   Step 2. Take a small section of hair from the outside of one section, and cross it over to the inside of the opposite section. The smaller the section of hair you cross over, the more intricate the finished braid will look.

Figure 1.130   Step 3. Take a section from the outside of the opposite section of hair and cross it over to the inside of the first section. Continue working from side to side until you reach the bottom of the braid. Secure the bottom of the braid with an elastic band.

Figure 1.131   Step 4. The finished fishtail/herringbone braid.

Basic French Twist

One other styling skill that is very useful to know how to do is the basic French twist. Many of the styles in this book incorporate a French twist as a part of the finished style. A French twist is an elegant way to get all of the hair up to the crown of the head.

Figure 1.132   Step 1. Sweep all of the hair in the back of the wig off to one side. Secure the hair with a row of interlocking bobby pins going up the center of the head.

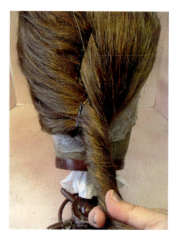

Figure 1.133   Step 2. Gather all of the hair in your hand and twist it.

Figure 1.134   Step 3. Pull the twisted hair up alongside the row of bobby pins.

Figure 1.135   Step 4. Pull the twisted base of the ponytail up over the ponytail.

Figure 1.136   Step 5. Secure the roll by tucking and pinning bobby pins all along the roll.

Figures 1.137 and 1.138   Step 6. What you do with the loose ends of the hair will depend on the style you are creating. Here, I simply rolled the ends under to form a curl that completes the French twist.

Using Your Own Hair

All of the styles in this book could be done on a real person's hair if it was the appropriate length. Obviously, you cannot pin rollers directly into a living person's head, but you can recreate the setting pattern with plastic rollers that are allowed to dry overnight or under a bonnet hair dryer (as you might see in a hair salon), with hot rollers, or with a curling iron. Pin curls (secured with clips or hairpins) and braids can also be done on real hair. One thing to keep in mind when styling real hair is that you will need the same supplies readily available to you as you would for styling wigs. If the set illustrated is done with 20 rollers, trying to achieve it with six hot rollers of the wrong size is not realistic. Also keep in mind that many historical hairstyles were either wigs or they incorporated hairpieces. You may also need to use added hairpieces

to achieve the look you are aiming for. These hairpieces would need to be styled in advance of styling the person's hair, using the techniques outlined in this chapter (waving, curling, or braiding.)

Breaking Down/Putting Together a Hairstyle

Once you have mastered all of the basic styling techniques, you must figure out how to put them all together to make a hairstyle. Following the steps for each period in this book will give you a good starting point, but you will want to do variations for each period in order to ensure that you do not create a production full of clones.

The best way to approach putting together a hairstyle is to break the style down into five sections: the front, the left side, the right side, the crown, and the nape. If you examine what each section of hair needs to look like, it becomes much easier to form a plan of attack for the hairstyle. For example, let's look at this detail of a hairstyle from Sandro Botticelli's painting *Primavera* (Figure 1.139). By breaking this style down into sections (Figure 1.140), you can begin to plan how you might style a wig in this hairstyle.

Figure 1.139   Botticelli's painting *Primavera*.

Figure 1.140   The Botticelli hairstyle broken down into sections.

The top/front of the hairstyle (A) is very flat with a center part. The side sections (B) have a tighter, wavier curl. This look could be achieved by setting this section of the hair on dime-sized rollers set in spiral curls. Setting these curls with drag at the roots would help keep section A flat and without much volume. The crown of the wig (C) is also flat, with the ends of the hair going into large, soft curls. There is also a small braid (D) over the crown of the head. At the nape of the neck (E), the large soft curls continue from the crown of the head. These large soft curls in sections C and E could be achieved by setting the hair on quarter-sized rollers, set off base with drag. Figure 1.141 shows a recreation of this hairstyle styled and modeled by Josephine McAdam, where she has added an additional small switch of hair in order to create the braid circling the crown of the head.

Figure 1.141   Student Josephine McAdam models her version of Botticelli's hairstyle.

Always refer back to your period research and ask yourself, "Is this section of the hair curly?"; "Are there ringlets hanging down in the back?"; "Should the bun be at the crown of the head or at the nape?" and other similar questions in order to figure out the hairstyle.

Hairstyling Tips

Some other tips for putting together a successful hairstyle:

1. Do not try to make your hairstyle too perfect. Wigs look better when they have a slightly more natural look. Humans aren't perfect, and their hair is rarely perfect either. This is not an excuse to style the hair sloppily. Rather, think about putting the style together in a realistic way—real people have hairs that are a bit out of place or not perfectly curled.

2. Have a small bit of the hair break the hairline of the wig somewhere. We rarely see every bit of someone's hairline. Adding little wisps and tendrils helps to both disguise the fact that the hair is a wig and makes the style look more natural.

3. Hairnets are your friend! Use hairnets to secure sections of a hairstyle in place. This will make the section hold better, look neater, and cut down on wig maintenance.

4. The wig will look more natural if it reveals the shape of the skull somewhere. It does not need to be a large section of hair that is plastered down to the head. Rather, even the smallest section of the style that is close to the head will make the wig look more realistic. There are exceptions to this rule—1960s hairstyles, for example, do not generally hug the head anywhere (maybe this is why 60s' hair often looks so wiggy!)

5. Consider the weight and balance of the wig as you style. A wig that is extremely top heavy or back heavy will be uncomfortable for the performer who has to wear it. Also consider whether the wig will need to be worn with a hat or headpiece. Try the hat or headpiece on the wig as you are styling it in order to be sure everything works together.

6. The audience does not wish to see all of the effort that went into styling your wig. Do not overwork the wig so much that it looks like a product-encrusted, tortured wig held together with a hundred carefully placed bobby pins. A proper set and careful hiding of pins will go a long way toward making the hairstyle look graceful.

7. Consider the character. The hair on a character's head says a lot about who they are. It reveals things like social status, environment, and personality. As a wig designer, you can help the actor develop his or her character by making appropriate hair choices. Is the character a buttoned-up librarian whose hair has not moved in 20 years? Is she a social climber whose hair is ridiculously overdone? Is he a Restoration-era fop who slavishly follows every trend of the day? Make good choices so that the audience knows exactly who the character is.

8. Period is in the silhouette; character is in the details. The overall shape of the hairstyle will let the audience know the period in which the play or film is taking place. The details within that hairstyle determine the character. This includes not only the details of the style itself, but also the details of the hair decorations.

Tips for Using this Book

In each chapter, I have discussed basic looks for each period, including period research. For each major period in fashion history, I have taken you through the steps to create at least one hairstyle representative of that period. Sometimes the style will be a direct copy of a particular reference picture; other styles will be ones I have created by combining several references in order to show you specific techniques. I will note which reference I am working from when applicable. As you become more comfortable with wig styling, you will begin to be able to create different hairstyles based on the basic techniques that are discussed. I have listed in each chapter ideas about variations on these styles. I have also included at the beginning of each chapter a list of artists, designers, and style icons/important people to help get you started on your research into each period.

In the styling examples, I use rollers that are the same size in diameter, but different colors. Different colors do not have any significance in the styling—they just happen to be the colors of the rollers I have. I also do not make any distinction between spring wire rollers or plastic rollers—I use them interchangeably. I will note the size of roller you need to use in order to make the instructions clearer.

For almost every wig style I style, I set a small tendril of hair on a pencil-sized (or smaller) roller in front of the ear (Figure 1.142). I also often (especially when styling an updo) set short tendrils or curls around the nape of the wig, starting back behind the ears (Figure 1.143). These small wispy curls help both hard front wigs and lace front wigs look more realistic by camouflaging the edge of the wig.

Figure 1.142   A tendril of hair set in front of the ear in the sideburn area of the wig.

Figure 1.143   Tendrils of hair set at the nape of the neck and behind the ears help conceal the back edge of the wig.

For most of the styling examples, I use lace front wigs because they are the ideal choice. If you do not have lace front wigs, you can still create most of the styles in this book. You can adapt wigs in many ways—you can add wefting to them to add volume or length, and you can incorporate hairpieces in order to add to the style of your wig. If you are using a hard front wig, you may need to take extra steps in order to conceal the front edge of the wig. For example, you may need to set additional small tendrils of hair going forward onto the forehead. Other styles have the hair coming onto the face in such a way that the hairline would be covered already. Still other styles are from historical periods where wigs would have been worn, so the wig looking like a wig instead of like natural hair is not an issue. Look carefully at the wigs you have available to you and the style you are trying to create in order to make good choices about what wig will work best for your project.

Practice all of the wig techniques, do a lot of historical period research, and think about your characters. You are now ready to begin creating period hairstyles. The following chapters will guide you through the basics of styling in periods throughout history. Good luck in making many fantastic creations!

two

EARLY VICTORIAN/ ROMANTIC

{ *1835–1860* }

Figure 2.1   Empress Eugènie (1826–1920) Surrounded by her Ladies-in-Waiting, 1855 (oil on canvas), Winterhalter, Franz Xaver (1805–73) / Chateau de Compiègne, Oise, France / Giraudon / The Bridgeman Art Library. This group portrait is an excellent example of a wide variety of Victorian era hairstyles.

Important Events

1837   Queen Victoria takes the throne of England

1837   Samuel Morse develops the telegraph

1839   Louis Daguerre and J.N. Nièpce co-invent daguerreotype photography

1845   Elias Howe invents the sewing machine

1845   Irish famine begins

1848   The Pre-Raphaelite Brotherhood is founded

1849   The American Gold Rush

1851   The Great Exhibition/the first World's Fair is held

1854   The Crimean War

Important Artists/Designers

William Blake, Dominique Ingres, John Everett Millais, Franz Winterhalter.

Important People/Style Icons

Prince Albert and Queen Victoria, Charles Dickens, Empress Eugenie, Franz Joseph I, Jenny Lind, Victoire de Nemours.

Victorian/Romantic Women

Following the excess and height of 1830 hairstyles, Victorian hairstyles became more subdued. Queen Victoria took the throne and her more conservative sensibilities set the tone for the fashions in her era. *Godey's Ladies Book* (1830–1878), a periodical that featured pictures of fashions and hairstyles, was also exerting great influence over popular fashion. The high buns of the 1830s moved down to the back of the head.

Figure 2.2   Profile of a Young Lady, c.1840 (coloured chalks on paper), English School, (19th century) / Private Collection / © Charles Plante Fine Arts / The Bridgeman Art Library. This portrait shows both the lower bun placement of this era, and also the fashion of looping hair around the ears.

The area of hair around a lady's ears was a particular focal point in this era. The hair might be braided or coiled and looped around the ears, as in Figure 2.2. The ears also might be entirely covered with long ringlets, as in Figure 2.3. These ringlets might consist of looser curls, or they might be defined columns of hair known as sausage curls.

Figure 2.4   Portrait of Annie Gambart (oil on canvas), Frith, William Powell (1819–1909) / Private Collection / © Christopher Wood Gallery, London, UK / The Bridgeman Art Library.

Figure 2.3   Portrait of Julia Cartwright, Richmond, George (1809–96) / Private Collection / The Bridgeman Art Library. This portrait is a lovely example of long ringlets that frame the face.

Figure 2.5   This portrait photograph shows a woman's hair that has been smoothed over her ears and pulled into a coiled bun at the back of her head.

Hair in this period was still parted in the center. More simple styles can also be found in this period, with hair simply being smoothed down from a center part, and then smoothed back to cover the ears. Figures 2.4 and 2.5 are examples of this style. Sometimes the hair was puffed out over the ears to add volume to the sides of the hair (see Figure 2.4). This helped visually balance the head with the large hoop skirts women were wearing at this time.

It was also very important at this time for a woman's hair to look shiny and healthy. Figures 2.1 and 2.4 are good examples of shining hair. Pomades and oils were used to heighten this effect.

Victorian/Romantic Men

Men's hair in the Victorian era was becoming longer on top, so that it could be formed into romantic windswept curls and waves. These hairstyles often had a deep side part.

Figure 2.7   Fashion plate depicting male clothing, published by 'La Fashion', 1841 (colour litho), French School (19th century) / Musée de la Ville de Paris, Musée Carnavalet, Paris, France / Giraudon / The Bridgeman Art Library.

Figure 2.6   Daguerreotype of George Peter Alexander Healy, circa 1850. This portrait photograph shows off a longer men's hairstyle with a deep side part in the hair.

Popular public figures such as Charles Dickens gave face to the curled styles and well groomed facial hair of the period, as seen in Figure 2.8.

Figure 2.8   Albumen photograph of Charles Dickens, circa 1860s, seated in an armchair and looking to his left, circa 1860s. Heritage Auction Gallery.

Men's facial hair was still enjoying great popularity at this time. All sorts of styles were fashionable, including dramatic sideburns, neat mustaches, and long square goatees. Men's hair was also expected to be shiny at this time.

Victorian/Romantic Woman's Styling—
Step by Step Instructions

I based this hairstyle on the woman at the far left side of Figure 2.1 (wearing the rose pink dress).

Figure 2.9   Step 1. Begin with a wig that is long (16 inches long at the nape of the neck) and mostly all one length. There could be some shorter layers (10 inches long) around the face. Here, I used a lace front synthetic wig.

Figure 2.10   Step 2. Part the hair in the center with a rat tail comb. Next, pin blocking tape around the top of the head a few inches away from the part. This will help keep the hair in the front section of the wig flat and smooth.

Figure 2.11   Step 3. Set three sausage curls on the top row on each side of the head, rolling towards the face. For the second, lower row, set one sausage curl rolling away from the face. Use dime-sized rollers for all of these curls. Also set a small tendril rolling towards the face.

Figure 2.12   Step 4. Pull most of the rest of the hair in the wig into a ponytail at the back of the head. Leave a section of hair hanging loose at the nape of the neck.

Figure 2.13   Step 5. Set the hair in the ponytail on three nickel-sized rollers.

Figure 2.14   Step 6. Pull the hair at the nape of the neck into a second, lower ponytail. You will then roll the hair in the low ponytail onto four nickel-sized rollers.

Victorian Woman's Hairstyle—The Finished Set

Figures 2.15–18 The finished Victorian Woman's style set.

Once you have finished setting the wig, steam each roller thoroughly if the wig is made of synthetic hair. If the wig is human hair, soak each roller with water sprayed from a spray bottle. After steaming or wetting, place the wig in a wig dryer for 75 minutes.

To style:

Figure 2.19   Step 7. Remove all of the rollers in the wig, beginning at the nape of the neck. Take extra care when you unwind the ringlets at the sides of the face.

Figure 2.20   Step 8. Brush the hair in the top ponytail around your fingers to form four looped curls. Pin two of these curls in place with bobby pins.

Figure 2.21   Step 9. Bring the second two curls up and on top of the first two curls you pinned in place. Use your fingers to arrange the curls in a pretty way and pin them in place.

Figure 2.22   Step 10. Snip through the rubber band holding the lower ponytail. This will allow you to get rid of the rubber band without tangling the hair.

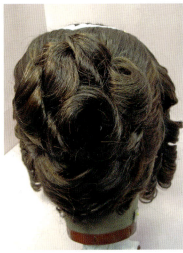

Figure 2.23   Step 11. Divide the hair at the nape of the neck in half. Drape each half section up the back of the head, and pin it on the side of the bun. (The lower left section should be pulled up and pinned on the right side of the bun, and the lower right section should be pulled up and pinned to the left side of the bun.)

Figure 2.24   Step 12. Brush each loose section of hair around your finger to form another curl. Pin these curls in place and incorporate them into the bun. You can cover the bun with a hairnet to make it even more secure and neat.

Figure 2.25   Step 13. Move to the ringlets in the front of the hairstyle. Brush through each ringlet section with a teasing/smoothing brush.

Figure 2.26   Step 14. Brush each sausage curl around a dowel rod, then slide the dowel rod out of the curl. Misting the hair with hairspray before you brush it around the dowel rod will help the ringlet stay in place even better. Be sure not to put so much hairspray on the section that it sticks to the dowel rod.

Figure 2.27   Step 15. If the bottom of the ringlet begins to separate, use your finger to push the bottom bit of hair up inside the rest of the ringlet.

Victorian Woman—The Completed Hairstyle

Figures 2.28–31   The completed Victorian Woman's style. Photography: Tim Babiak. Model: Sabrina Lotfi.

Variations

To create variety in your Victorian/Romantic women's hairstyles, follow the examples in Figure 2.1. Some of the hairstyles in that painting have ringlets around the face, some have the hair smoothed back over the ears. Some of the styles have buns only in the back, while some of the styles have a few ringlets hanging down. Some of the hairstyles are decorated with ribbons, some with flowers. You can also dress the hair in loops or braids around the ears.

Victorian Man's Styling—Step by Step Instructions

This hairstyle is based on a combination of the styles seen in Figures 2.6 and 2.8.

 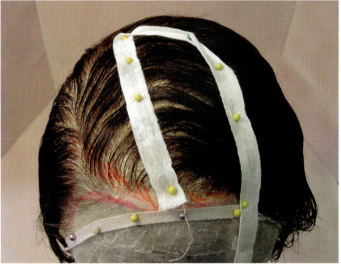

Figure 2.32   Step 1. Begin with a short wig that has longer hair (at least 5 inches long) on top, and shorter hair in the back and nape areas. A fully ventilated, human hair lace wig is best for this kind of hairstyle. I used a fully ventilated lace front wig made of human hair.

Figure 2.33   Step 2. Make a deep side part in the wig with a comb. Saturate the top section of the wig with setting lotion. Form a flat wave on the top of the wig by combing the hair away from the face and pinning the center of the wave with a piece of blocking tape. Next, comb the hair towards the face to form the second half of the wave, and pin it in place with the blocking tape.

Figure 2.34   Step 3. Use dime-sized rollers to set curls at the end of the waved section of hair.

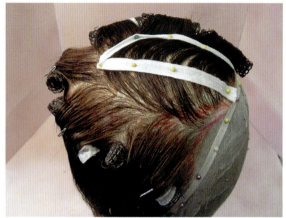

Figure 2.35   Step 4. Continue working your way around the head with dime-sized rollers.

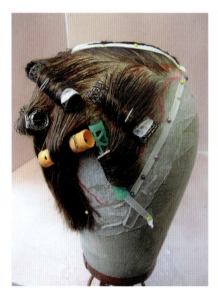

Figure 2.36   Step 5. Drop down to the next row of rollers. Set the first roller (pencil-sized) going away from the face in the temple/sideburn area. The rest of the row should be rolled towards the ears on dime-sized rollers.

Figure 2.37   Step 6. Continue setting the wig on decreasing sizes of rollers, ending on small perm rods. Also alternate the rows in diagonal directions. Do not worry if some of the hair is too short to fit around a roller. We will curl this hair by hand later.

Victorian Man's Hairstyle—The Finished Set

Figures 2.38–41 The finished Victorian Man's style set.

Once you have finished setting the wig, steam each roller thoroughly if the wig is made of synthetic hair. If the wig is human hair, soak each roller with water sprayed from a spray bottle. After steaming or wetting, place the wig in a wig dryer for 75 minutes.

To style:

Figure 2.42   Step 7. Remove all of the rollers from the wig, beginning at the nape of the neck.

Figure 2.43   Step 8. Use a large brush to thoroughly brush through all of the hair in the wig.

Figure 2.44   Step 9. Go back into the wig with a rat tail comb. Use the comb to smooth out the waves and curls in the hairstyle and to push them into place.

Figure 2.45   Step 10. Use duckbill clips to hold the waves in place. Mist this section with hairspray.

Figure 2.46   Step 11. Plug in a Marcel oven and allow it to heat up. A Marcel oven is a small oven that you place metal curling irons inside. This heats them to very high temperatures. Marcel irons come in very small sizes that make them ideal for styling short lengths of hair. Once it becomes warm, place a couple of small Marcel irons inside. Once the irons are hot, test them on a scrap piece of human hair in order to ensure that they will not scorch the hair. *Always test a Marcel iron's heat before using it on a wig!* Marcel irons should never be used on a synthetic hair wig—they will scorch the hair beyond repair. If you are using a synthetic wig, style the short hair by rolling it on a bobby pin if the hair is long enough. If the hair is not long enough, comb the short hairs in the direction you wish for them to go, spray them with hairspray, and allow them to set overnight.

Figures 2.47 and 2.48 Step 12. Use the Marcel irons to curl any bits of hair that have not already been curled.

Figure 2.49 Step 13. Use a regular electric curling iron to curl small sections of hair at the front of the wig. Letting a small section of the hair fall in front of the hairline will help the wig look much more natural.

Figure 2.50 Step 14. Use the curling iron on the longer side of the part to curl the hair up and away from the face.

Figure 2.51 Step 15. Brush through the hair that you have just curled so that it forms a sweeping flip up. You can add facial hair to your performer—here, I added a pair of mutton chops to complete the final look.

Victorian Man—The Completed Hairstyle

Figures 2.52–55   The completed Victorian Man's style. Photography: Tim Babiak. Model: Leslie Hethcox.

Variations

Experiment with different lengths of hair to create men's look for this period. The hair might be longer and smoother, or shorter and curlier. Change up the facial hair looks to really play up the differences in this period—make good use of various sizes and styles of sideburns, mustaches, and goatees.

three

CIVIL WAR ERA/
LATE VICTORIAN

{ *1860–1885* }

Figure 3.1   Hairstyles with ribbons, illustration from 'La Mode Illustrée', 1872 (colour engraving), Toudouze, Anais (or Colin, Adèle Anaïs) (1822–99) / Bibliothèque des Arts Decoratifs, Paris, France / Archives Charmet / The Bridgeman Art Library International

Important Events

1860	The American Civil War begins
1862	*Les Miserables*, by Victor Hugo, is published.
1865	Abraham Lincoln is assassinated by John Wilkes Booth
1870	Napoleon III is overthrown
1873	Levi Strauss sells the first pairs of blue jeans
1876	Alexander Graham Bell patents the telephone
1881	Tsar Alexander II is assassinated in Russia

Important Artists/Designers

Edward Burne-Jones, Honoré Daumier, Edgar Degas, Edouard Manet, Claude Monet, Camille Pissarro, Pierre Auguste Renoir, Dante Gabriel Rosetti, Charles Frederick Worth.

Important People/Style Icons

Empress Elisabeth of Austria, Jesse James, Lily Langtry, Franz Liszt, Queen Victoria.

Late Victorian Women

Women's hair in the Civil War/ late Victorian era became more simple and sedate. The ringlets of hair worn around the face fell out of fashion in favor of styles that were center parted and smoothly rolled back away from the face. The ears were also being exposed again for the first time in decades.

Figure 3.2 Miss Elinor Guthrie, by Frederic Leighton (circa 1865). In this portrait, the subject's simple hairstyle is swept away from her face, exposing her ears.

At the nape of the neck, the hair was pulled into a heavy roll. The crown of the head was usually left smooth. The roll of hair on the nape was sometimes contained by a snood (a decorative hair net).

Figure 3.3 A photograph of a hairstyle from the 1860s featuring a snood as a part of the style.

The clean, rounded shapes of the hairstyles complemented the full hoop skirts of the dresses from that era. Later in this era, the fullness in the skirts shifted to the back of the dresses as the bustle became a popular fashion. Just as the fashion became more streamlined on the sides, so did the hairstyles. The hair became very tight on the sides and the fullness moved up to the top of the head. In many ways, the silhouette of the time period made women resemble horses. The bustles gave the illusion of a second set of legs, and the shape of the hair was very like that of a horse's mane.

Figure 3.4 An 1870s fashion plate from *Victoria*, illustrating the bustle silhouette of the gowns and the sleeker, horse like hairstyles.

For daytime, the hair was sleek on the sides with a simple high bun. In 1872, French hairdresser Marcel Grateau pioneered a technique of using hot tongs to semi-permanently wave hair. Soon, people all over Europe were seeking to have their hair styled in this fashion. The deep waves created by this technique were incorporated into hairstyles of this time in a variety of ways. The heat from this type of styling was hard on the hair, however. Looking at photographs of women from this time often reveals hair that has taken on a frizzed, fried texture.

Figure 3.5 Hairstyles illustrated in *Godey's Lady's Book and Magazine,* are examples of a more daytime look from this era. Notice the slightly frizzed, waved texture present in the hair.

For evening affairs, the hair was dressed very high on the top of the head with long ringlets hanging down the back. The hairstyles would be elaborately decorated with ribbons and flowers, such as those shown in Figure 3.1 at the beginning of this chapter. Large braids, barrel rolls, and coils were often wrapped around the top and crown of the head. Several different things could be happening at the center front of the hairstyle. It could be simply parted in the center and pulled back, such as in the figure on the bottom left of Figure 3.1. The style could have a small, tightly Marcel waved section at the center front, such as on the figure at the top right side of Figure 3.1. A third option was for the hair to be arranged in a clump of small tight curls at the center front, such as in figure 3.6.

Figure 3.6 The woman in this photograph has a section of tight curls at the center front, a cluster of shaped rolls on top, and long ringlets hanging down in the back of her hairstyle.

Figure 3.7 Ten illustrations of different types of wigs and hair pieces from a French magazine.
May 1875.

Because these styles were so elaborate, they required a greater amount of hair than most people can grow. The use of artificial hairpieces became very common and necessary to achieve this fashion. Large tortoiseshell combs were also very popular during this time period.

Late Victorian Men

Men's hairstyles at this time are slightly shorter than found in the previous decades. They still often had a deep side part, sometimes with an asymmetrical pouf on top.

Figure 3.9   Major General Ambrose Everett Burnside, from *The History of the United States*, Vol. II. by Charles Mackay, engraved by T.W. Hunt from a photograph (engraving), American School, (19th century) / Private Collection / The Bridgeman Art Library International.

Figure 3.8   Canadian legislator John Charles Rykert wears a hairstyle with a deep side part with an asymmetrical flip in the front.

This era continued the heyday of extravagance in men's facial hair. In the 1860s, American general Ambrose Burnside wore a distinctive fashion of facial hair. His look consisted of full side whiskers that were connected by a mustache. Side whiskers are now often referred to as sideburns in reference to his name.

Almost any variation on facial hair can be found in this period if one looks hard enough. Figure 3.10 shows a beard that exists under the chin only. The man in Figure 3.8 has bristly side whiskers, but no mustache or chin hair.

Figure 3.10   Portrait photograph of John Tyndall (1820–93) Irish physicist (photo), / The Royal Institution, London, UK / The Bridgeman Art Library International.

Whatever the late Victorian era man's facial hair choice might be, it was shown off to advantage by the high collars and elaborate neckwear of the period.

1870s/ Late Victorian Woman's Styling— Step by Step Instructions

This wig was inspired by the style in Figure 3.6, with the small, tightly waved bangs seen on a couple of the styles in Figure 3.1.

Figure 3.11 Step 1. Begin with a wig that is long (at least 16 inches at the nape of the neck) with a generous amount of hair. A wig with bangs also works well for this style. The wig in this picture is synthetic hair with a lace front.

Figure 3.12 Step 2. Make a clean center part in the front section of the hair.

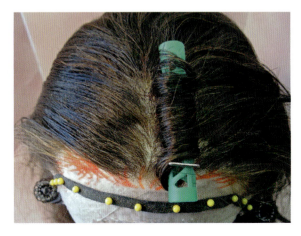

Figure 3.13 Step 3. Set the front section on base on small, pencil-sized rollers, rolling away from the center part.

Figure 3.14 Step 4. Set two rollers on either side of the center part.

Late Victorian Woman's Hairstyle—The Finished Set

Figures 3.23–26   The finished 1870s Late Victorian Woman's set, viewed from all angles.

Once you have finished setting the wig, steam it if it is synthetic. If it is human hair, through spray the hair with water. Put the wig in the wig dryer after you have finished steaming and/or spraying, and dry it for 75 minutes.

To style the wig:

Figure 3.27   Step 13. To style, remove all of the rollers, beginning at the nape of the wig. Carefully unwind the sausage curls.

Figure 3.28   Step 14. The wig, with all of the rollers removed.

Figure 3.29   Step 15. Use a wire teasing comb to pick through and fluff the hair at the center front section of the wig. This will break up the curls and help to hide any roller breaks you may have.

Figure 3.30   Step 16. Next, brush through and smooth this section of hair with a teasing/smoothing brush.

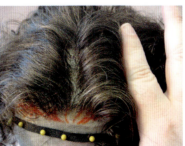

Figure 3.31   Step 17. Push the small waves in this section into shape with your fingers.

Figure 3.32   Step 18. Pin blocking tape in place to help you hold and shape these waves.

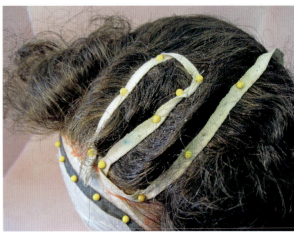

Figure 3.33   Step 19. Use a rat tail comb to push the waves into place and to create ridges between each crest of the wave.

Figure 3.34   Step 20. The full wave, pinned in place and sprayed with hairspray.

Figure 3.35   Step 21. Shape the ends of the hair from the section by brushing them into small curls around your finger.

Figure 3.36   Step 22. Arrange the small curls in place and secure with a bobby pin.

Figure 3.37 Step 23. Move down to the side sections of the wig. Brush through these sections with your teasing/smoothing brush.

Figure 3.38 Step 24. Secure the side sections near the base of the ponytail with crossed bobby pins.

Figure 3.39 Step 25. Move to the crown of the head. Brush through this entire section of hair with your teasing/ smoothing brush and gather all of the hair into your hand.

Figure 3.40 Step 26. Pin a small hair rat at the middle on the crown of the head. Secure the rat with bobby pins.

Figure 3.43 Step 29. Ringlets pinned on both sides of the hair rat.

Figure 3.41 Step 27. Form some of the hair underneath the rat into a large ringlet.

Figure 3.42 Step 28. Drape the hair in the ringlet up alongside the hair rat. Fold it in half and pin the ringlet in the center. Pin the other half of the ringlet back down in the direction you started from.

Figure 3.44 Step 30. Take a small section of hair from the ponytail in the back of the wig, form it into a ringlet, and use it to cover the rest of the small rat.

Figure 3.45 Step 31. Brush through the rest of the hair in the ponytail, and roll it up in a second rat or hair pad.

Figure 3.46 Step 32. Turn the hair rat that has been rolled with hair sideways and pin it so that it sits vertically along the back of the head.

Figure 3.47 Step 33. The roll, pinned in place with large wig pins. The hair has been adjusted so that the entire rat is covered.

Figure 3.48 Step 34. Comb the hair from the side sections into ringlets.

Figure 3.49 Step 35. Pin these ringlets on either side of the roll.

Figure 3.50 Step 36. Finished view of the ringlets pinned in place.

Figures 3.51 and 3.52 Step 37. Continue shaping the hair in the back into ringlets and arranging them in a pretty way.

Figure 3.55 Step 40. If the ends of your ringlets stick out irregularly, push the end of the ringlet up into itself with your finger.

Figure 3.53 Step 38. To form the long sausage curls hanging down in the back, use a dowel rod to brush the curls around. Once you remove the rod, you will have a nice smooth curl.

Figure 3.54 Step 39. The ringlets hanging down in the back of the wig, once they have been smoothed and formed into shape.

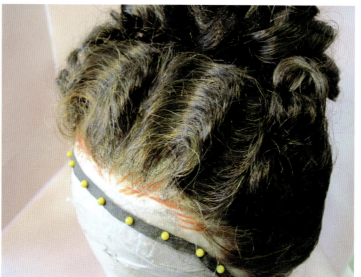

Figure 3.56 Step 41. When you are ready for the wig to be worn, remove the blocking tape that was holding the waves in place in the front of the wig.

Figure 3.57 Step 42. Add some decorative accents to complete the period look of this wig.

Late Victorian Woman—The Completed Hairstyle

Figures 3.58–61   The completed 1870s Late Victorian Woman's style. Photography: Tim Babiak. Model: Ivy Negron.

Variations

For styles from the early part of this era, you could do any number of variations of a wig with a center part and waves or rolls smoothed back above the ears. In the back, these wigs could either be styled ringlets, rolls, or caught up in a snood.

In the later part of this era, there are many possibilities for variety just in the decoration alone.

Experiment with ribbons, flowers, combs, birds, and jewels to create many different looks. You can also use variety in the center front of the wig. You can do either small sculpted finger waves (such as in the demonstrated style) or you can do a cluster of tight frizzled curls, such as in Figure 3.62.

Figures 3.62 and 3.63   Juliet Robb models a late Victorian wig styled by Thumper Gosney. Notice the section of small tight curls in the center front of the wig.

four

THE GAY NINETIES

{ *1885–1901* }

Figure 4.1   Portrait of Princess Alexandra (1844–1925) of Denmark (b/w photo), Downey, W. and D. (fl.1860–1905) / Archives Larousse, Paris, France / Giraudon / The Bridgeman Art Library International.

1890s Women

The Gay Nineties was a time of perceived prosperity and increased physical activity. These were the last years of Queen Victoria's reign, before the chaos of World War I would send the world into a tailspin. Clothing became simpler—the bustles and hoopskirts of the previous period had fallen out of fashion (corsets were still very much a part of a woman's daily wardrobe, however.) The idea of sportswear becomes important for one of the first times in history. Clothing became more tailored; likewise, hairstyles also became a bit simpler. Hair was

Important Events

1886	The Statue of Liberty is constructed
1888	The Jack the Ripper murders occur in Whitechapel
1891	Sir Arthur Conan Doyle publishes the first Sherlock Holmes story
1892	Tchaikovsky's *Nutcracker Suite* premieres
1895	Oscar Wilde's *The Importance of Being Earnest* premieres
1898	The Spanish–American War is fought
1901	Death of Queen Victoria

Important Artists/Designers

Aubrey Beardsley, Paul Cézanne, Paul Gauguin, George Seurat, John Singer Sargent, Henri de Toulouse-Lautrec, John William Waterhouse, James McNeil Whistler

Important People/Style Icons

Princess Alexandra, Sarah Bernhardt, Mrs. Patrick Campbell, Annie Oakley, Ellen Terry, Oscar Wilde

often grown extremely long, and was considered to be a woman's crowning glory. Women were still wearing their hair piled high on their head, but unlike the previous period, the shape was much more basic. Hair would often be waved, and then pulled up on top of the head in a French twist. Some women favored a simple topknot on the top of their head. Other women chose to coil their hair around on the top of the head, creating a large bun that was almost the same width as the head itself. Fashionable women's blouses were often high necked at this time, so a woman's hair was usually pulled up off of the neck.

Figure 4.2 This 1890s photograph of a woman shows her hair pulled up into a rather simple high bun.

Figure 4.3   The Vicomtesse De Montmorand, painted by James Joseph Jacques Tissot in 1889, wears her hair coiled on top of her head in a wide, flat bun.

Grey hair, surprisingly, was very much in vogue at this time. Many women were using hair powders (used to absorb grease and create a soft look), which likely contributed to the trend of fashionable grey hair. The practice of curling hair with hot Marcel irons was still all the rage at this time. As a result, many women had damaged hair from the high temperatures of the curling irons. Photographs of women at this time often show the hair looking slight fuzzy and flyaway. Tightly curled or "frizzled" bangs were extremely popular at this time. Women would use the curling irons to painstaking curl a fringe of bangs. Examples of these bangs can be seen in Figures 4.1 and 4.4.

Figure 4.4   This photograph of a woman is an example of a simple 1890s hairstyle with a tightly curled fringe.

Evening hairstyles for women were often more elaborate and complicated. The twists and curls on top of the head would be more elaborate, and hairpieces might be used to add volume or interest. These hairstyles might incorporate jewels, fancy combs, or plumes.

Figure 4.5   Hair-dressing, *Harper's Bazaar*, 16 January 1892. The magazine feature shows off an evening hairstyle, complete with pre-made artificial bun.

1890s Men

Men in the 1890s were quite dapper. They were still wearing their hair cut short and close to the head. It was often styled with a very clean part (either in the center or on the side), held in place with hair grease or pomade. Facial hair in this period was very dramatic. Men often grew large, elaborate mustaches that became a focal point of their look.

Figure 4.7   Portrait of Paul Wayland Bartlett, by Charles Sprague Pearce, 1890. This portrait is an example of a small, fashionable 1890s goatee.

The Aesthetic Dress movement influenced fashions for both men and women. The emphasis in clothing was on simple lines and luxurious fabrics. Hairstyles favored by Aesthetics were also more simple and flowing; they rejected the tightly bound updos and severe men's short haircuts of the time.

HAAKON VII

Figure 4.6   King Haakon VII of Norway (1872–1957), early 20th century (colour litho), French School, (20th century) / Musée de la Ville de Paris, Musée Carnavalet, Paris, France / Archives Charmet / The Bridgeman Art Library International. This photograph shows a neat, short haircut and an elaborate mustache.

This mustache might be styled in a walrus shape, or it might be waxed into a handlebar. Small pointy beards or goatees were also fashionable for men.

Figure 4.8   Oscar Wilde in his "aesthetic lecturing costume". Photograph by Napoleon Sarony, New York, early January 1882. Note how Wilde's hair is much longer and looser than the styles worn by other men in this era.

1890s Woman's Styling—Step by Step Instructions

This hairstyle is modeled after the one in the portrait in Figure 4.3.

Figure 4.9   Step 1. Begin with a long wig (at least 16 inches at the nape of the neck) that has a section of shorter hair or bangs (3 to 5 inches long) in the front. I used a long synthetic lace front wig for this style.

Figure 4.10   Step 2. Set the bangs on small perm rods, rolling towards the face.

Figure 4.11   Step 3. Set several small pencil rollers along the hairline and behind the section of bangs. This will help add the frizzy texture commonly seen in hairstyles of this time period.

Figure 4.12   Step 4. Behind the pencil rollers, set a row of dime-sized rollers, still setting the rollers away from the face.

Figures 4.13 and 4.14   Step 5. You are now going to begin setting the hair on quarter-sized rollers. Make sure to set your rollers in a brick pattern—this will keep you from having large gaps in your hairstyle.

Figure 4.15   Step 6. Pull most of the hair in the back of the wig up out of the way in a twist. Make sure to leave a section of hair hanging down at the nape of the neck.

Figure 4.16   Step 7. Roll the hair at the nape of the neck on quarter-sized rollers, rolling the hair up towards the crown of the head.

Figure 4.17 Step 8. Roll the bottom section of hair on dime-sized rollers, again rolling upwards toward the crown of the head.

Figure 4.18 Step 9. Braid the hair in the back of the wig into two French braids. This will allow you to create texture in the hair without creating a lot of unnecessary volume.

Figure 4.19 Step 10. Roll the ends of the braids onto dime-sized rollers, and pin the braids out of the way at the front of the head.

1890s Woman's Hairstyle—The Finished Set

Figures 4.20–23 The finished 1890s Woman's style set.

Once you have finished setting the wig, steam each roller thoroughly if the wig is made of synthetic hair. If the wig is human hair, soak each roller with water sprayed from a spray bottle. After steaming or wetting, place the wig in a wig dryer for 75 minutes.

To style:

Figure 4.24   Step 11. Begin removing all of the rollers, starting at the nape of the wig. Unbraid the braided section of hair. For now, leave the bang section of hair set on perm rods in the rollers.

Figure 4.25   Step 12. Brush through all of the hair with a large hairbrush.

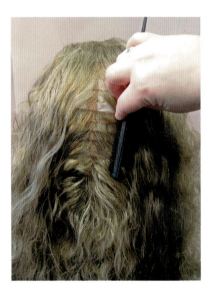

Figure 4.26   Step 13. Use a rat tail comb to make a center part in the back of the wig.

Figure 4.27   Step 14. Take half of the hair in your hand and twist the entire section of hair. Once twisted, twist the hair up the center back in order to create half of a French twist, leaving the ends loose. Make sure not to pull the twist so tight that you lose all of the texture in the hair. Pin the twist securely up the center back with bobby pins.

Figure 4.28 Step 15. Use a wire pick comb to smooth the hairs going into the twist. Once the hairs are in place, mist them in place with hairspray.

Figure 4.29 Step 16. Twist the hair on the other side of the wig to make a second French twist. The two twists should meet up in the center back of the wig.

Figure 4.30 Step 17. Divide the loose hair at the top of the twists into three sections. Brush one section of the hair around two fingers to form a large curl.

Figure 4.31 Step 18. Pin the curl so that it is relatively flat on the very top of the head.

Figure 4.32 Step 19. Form the other two sections of hair into curls, and pin them into place.

Figure 4.33 Step 20. Check your hairstyle from the front to make sure that it is symmetrical and that you are happy with the appearance of the curls.

Figure 4.34 Step 21. Remove the rollers from the bangs. Use a pick to separate the curls.

Figure 4.35 Step 22. Leave the curls a little bit frizzy. Use your fingers to arrange the curls in place. Pin them in place with bobby pins if necessary, making sure to hide the bobby pins.

Figure 4.36 Step 23. Use round head pins to arrange the curls. Mist with hairspray and let them sit overnight.

Figure 4.37 Step 24. To make the wig extra flat on the sides, use duckbill clips pinned into the waves. Again, mist the section with hairspray and let it sit overnight.

1890s Woman—The Completed Hairstyle

Figures 4.38–41 The completed 1890s Woman's style. Photography: Tim Babiak. Model: Sabrina Lotfi.

Variations

You can create variety in your 1890s hairstyles by making use of different textures of hair. While many women's hair had the frizzy textures caused by hot curling irons, other women still used pomades and oils to create very slick looking hair styles.

You can also create variety by playing around with the bang section. Besides the frizzy curled bangs, you can also find example of bangs with a center part and bangs with sculpted spit curls. Other women still held onto a simple center part with no bangs at all. Many of the buns in these hairstyles are placed very high on the top of the head, but you can also place the bun lower to create variety.

Later in this period, the hairstyles begin to gain the volume that will define the next period. You can make use of this volume to create more fashion forward character looks.

Figure 4.43   Notice how the hairstyle in this portrait is fuller on the sides than many styles from this period. This indicates that the hairstyle is from the later years of the 1890s.

Figure 4.42   The women in this portrait display a variety of 1890s bangs, hair texture, and bun placement.

five

EDWARDIAN ERA/ GIBSON GIRL

{ *1901–1910* }

Figures 5.4 and 5.5 Front and side views of Camille Clifford's signature hairstyle.

Figure 5.6 Camille Clifford models a typical Edwardian hat design that required voluminous hair for support.

To achieve these full hairstyles, women often needed to add pads, or "rats" to their hairstyles. Items known as "hair collectors" would sit on a woman's vanity. She would remove the loose hair from her hairbrush and insert it into the hole at the top of the hair collector. When the collector was full, the woman would remove the collected hair and use it to create stuffing that would add fullness to her hairstyle. In addition to being fashionable, hairstyles of this era also needed to be wide in order to support the large picture hats that were being worn. A popular hat design was the "Merry Widow" hat, which had piles of netting, feathers, and flowers.

In the majority of Edwardian hairstyles, the hair was pulled into a knot directly on the top of the head. Sometimes, however, a knot or coil of hair accentuated the nape of the neck (as in Figure 5.7). Still other women adopted the fashion of wearing part of their hair down, trailing over their shoulders (as in Figure 5.8).

Figures 5.7 and 5.8 Left: A coil of hair is just visible at the nape of this woman's neck. Right: This woman models the fashion of letting some long ringlets hang down over her shoulders.

Wavy textured hair was the most sought after during this period. Permanent waving machines were just being developed during this era—the early technology was a little terrifying! Women also explored some unusual hair products at this time to keep their crowning glories healthy and lustrous. Brilliantine, a hair oil, was used for shine, and some women even used a mercury ointment to keep their scalp healthy and prevent dandruff! Many miracle cures, guaranteed to cure anything from grey hair to baldness, could be found in the advertisements of the era.

Men, like women of the era, often used brilliantine to give their hair shine and hold it neatly in place. Macassar oil, an oil that was often made from coconut or palm oil, was also used during this era as a grooming and conditioning product. Because the oil had a tendency to travel from a man's hair onto the furniture he was resting his head against, people developed the antimacassar. This was a small crocheted cloth that was placed on the back of chairs to prevent the hair oil from sinking into the fabric of the furniture.

Edwardian Men

Men's hair in the Edwardian era was most often worn short, neat, and cleanly parted. Both side parts and center parts enjoyed popularity.

Figure 5.11   King Edward VII of England sports a very fashionable handlebar mustache and neatly trimmed, pointed beard in his coronation portrait.

Figures 5.9 and 5.10   Left: Theodore Roosevelt wears his hair slicked in place and neatly parted on the side. Right: William Randolph Hearst wore his hair neatly combed into a center part.

Figure 5.17   Step 5. Continue setting rollers at that angle down the other side of the hairline. A small tendril has been set in front of this ear as well.

Figure 5.18   Step 6. Behind the angled rollers at the center front hairline, set two rollers going back towards the crown.

Figure 5.20   Step 8. Next, set a second row of rollers going down from the crown.

Figure 5.19   Step 7. Work your way down and around the side of the wig, setting rollers going away from the hairline.

Figure 5.21   Step 9. Pull the hair at the crown and back of the head into a high ponytail. Make sure to leave at least 2 inches of hair around the back edges of the wig that is not pulled into the ponytail.

Figure 5.22 Step 10. Set the ponytail on nickel-sized rollers, in a circular pattern.

Figure 5.23 Step 11. Finish setting the hair in the ponytail—all of the rollers should be rolled away from the center of the ponytail.

Figure 5.24 Step 12. Roll all remaining hair in the wig up towards the crown. If there are short tendrils of hair around the back, set them on medium sized perm rods, such as the yellow perm rod used here.

Figure 5.25 Step 13. The finished view of the hair at the nape of the neck, rolled towards the crown of the head.

Gibson Girl Hairstyle—The Finished Set

Figures 5.26–29   The finished Gibson Girl style set, viewed from all angles.

Once you have finished setting the wig, steam it if it is synthetic. If it is human hair, through spray the hair with water. Put the wig in the wig dryer after you have finished steaming and/or spraying, and dry it for 75 minutes.

To style the wig:

Figure 5.30 Step 14. Remove all of the rollers beginning at the nape of the wig.

Figure 5.31 Step 15. Use a wide toothed comb to comb through all of the curls of the wig.

Figure 5.32 Step 16. After you comb through all of the curls, the wig will have a lot of volume.

Figure 5.33 Step 17. Use a large brush to brush through the hair at the nape of the wig. Use a duckbill clip to pin the hair in the ponytail out of your way.

Figure 5.34   Step 18. Divide the hair at the nape in half. Smooth half of the hair diagonally up the back of the wig.

Figure 5.35   Step 19. Secure the section of hair with crossed bobby pins next to the base of the ponytail.

Figure 5.36   Step 20. Spritz the section of hair you have just pinned with hairspray and smooth any flyaways with your teasing/smoothing brush.

Figure 5.37   Step 21. Smooth the other half of the hair at the nape of the neck diagonally up and over the other side of the wig. Secure with bobby pins next to the base of the ponytail. Spritz with hairspray and smooth down the stray hairs.

Figure 5.38   Step 22. Now turn to the front of the wig. Use the large brush to brush through all of the hair in the front section of the wig.

Figure 5.39   Step 23. Use the end of your teasing brush to separate out a small section of hair at the center front.

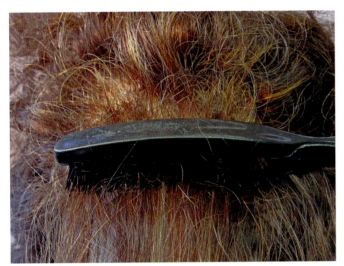

Figure 5.40 Step 24. Tease the hair to add volume and fullness at the front of the wig. Spray the hair lightly with hair spray after you finish teasing each section.

Figure 5.41 Step 25. Continue working your way down along the hairline towards the ear, teasing and spraying the hair as you go.

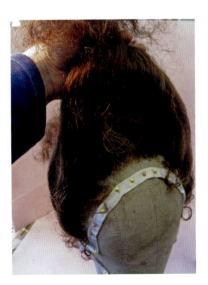

Figure 5.42 Step 26. After you have teased the entire front section of the wig, flip the hair back in the right direction and smooth the hair back. Spray with hairspray.

Figure 5.43 Step 27. Gather all of the front section of hair together in your hand. You may need to use a smoothing brush to help the hair sweep up in the right direction.

Figure 5.45   Step 29. Push the coiled hair down and forward. This will cause the hair to pouf out and form different shapes of wave in the front, depending on which direction you push.

Figure 5.46   Step 30. When you are satisfied with the way the volume and waves look in the front, pin the coil of hair in place.

Figure 5.44   Step 28. Gently twist the hair into a loose coil.

Figure 5.47   Step 31. Front view of the wig after the front section has been pinned in place.

Figure 5.48   Step 32. Use hairspray and a smoothing brush to tidy up and sections of flyaway hairs.

Figure 5.49   Step 33. You can adjust the volume or shape of the front by gently lifting sections with a teasing comb.

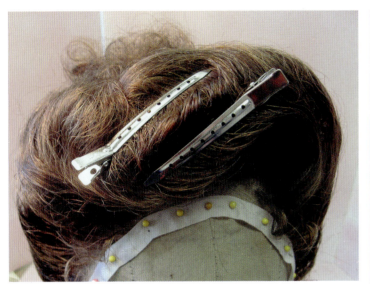

Figure 5.50   Step 34. I wanted to accentuate the wave in the front of this wig, so I used two duckbill clips to press the waves in place.

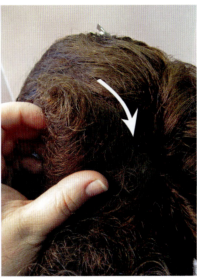

Figure 5.51   Step 35. Wind the end of the coiled hair into a cone shape. This will serve as the base for the high bun on your wig.

Figure 5.52   Step 36. Use a smoothing brush to smooth the pinned sections of hair from the nape of the wig around two fingers.

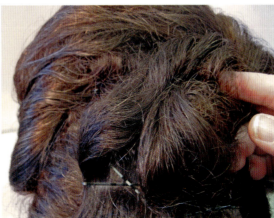

Figure 5.53   Step 37. Pin these curls you form in place, continuing to create the bun of the wig.

Figure 5.54   Step 38. Use the smoothing brush to comb sections of hair from the ponytail around two fingers.

Figure 5.55   Step 39. Continue pinning the curls of hair from the ponytail to finish off the bun of the hairstyle.

Figure 5.56   Step 40. Use a hairnet in a color that matches your wig. Pull the hairnet over the bun only.

Figure 5.57   Step 41. Pin the hairnet both around and within the curls of the bun so that it is completely hidden.

Figure 5.58   Step 42. The finished bun, with the hairnet pinned in place.

Gibson Girl—The Completed Hairstyle

Figures 5.59–62   The completed Gibson Girl style. Photography: Tim Babiak. Model: Ivy Negron.

Variations

There are several ways to great variety in your Gibson Girl looks. As you can see in Figure 5.70, the Gibson Girls display many differences in hair texture, bun placement, and the arrangement of the waves around the face.

Figure 5.63 In the reproduction of the Charles Dana Gibson drawing "The Weaker Sex", the women display multiple variations of the fashionable Edwardian looks.

Figure 5.64 The women of the "Scrubbing Club" wear some silhouettes that are more vertical and some that are more horizontal.

Varying the shape of the silhouette of the hair from wider hairstyles to hairstyles that are more vertical can also help you to produce a diverse looking production.

The most fashionable hair color of the era was a reddish chestnut brown (such as the hair color of Evelyn Nesbit), but all hair colors and textures can be used successfully in this period.

Figure 5.65 This wig, styled by Maur Sela, shows the rich, red-brown color so popular in the early 1900s.

six

THE TEENS

{ *1911–1920* }

Figure 6.1   A portrait photograph of a typical women's hairstyle of the Teens.

Important Events

1910	Ballet Russes performs *Scheherazade*, setting off a craze for Orientalism
1911	Triangle Shirtwaist Factory fire
1912	The *Titanic* strikes an iceberg and sinks on its maiden voyage
1914	Charlie Chaplin makes his first appearance as the Little Tramp character
1914–1919	World War I
1915	D.W. Griffith releases the film *Birth of a Nation*
1916	Norman Rockwell paints his first cover for the *Saturday Evening Post*
1917	Russian Revolution
1918	Czar Nicholas and his family are killed

Important Artists/Designers

Georges Braque, Marcel Duchamp, Wassily Kandinsky, Alphonse Mucha, Georgia O'Keefe, Paul Poiret, Norman Rockwell, Hans Unger.

Important People/Style Icons

Irene Castle, Coco Chanel, Charlie Chaplin, Isadora Duncan, Eleanora Duse, Douglas Fairbanks, Mary Pickford.

Women in the Teens

In the Teens, women were still expected to have great volumes of wavy hair that was then piled on their head. A permanent waving process was invented by Charles Nessler in 1905. He came to America in 1915 and opened a shop for waving hair. The hair was wrapped around brass rollers and hooked up to an electrical heating device. The process took 6 hours. The Art Nouveau and Orientalism movements also contributed to the romantic, exotic styles for women's hair. The volume of the hairstyles moves down the head so that the fullness was concentrated down around the ears, as in Figure 6.2, or on the back crown area of the head, as in Figure 6.3.

Figure 6.2 The hair in this photograph has been draped over the ears and arranged into a roll at the nape of the neck. The hair still has volume and width, but it is now lower on the head than in the first decade of the 20th century.

Figure 6.3   In this photograph, the hair has been dressed in elaborate rolls at the crown of the head.

Coronets of braids were popular at this time, as were piled masses of hair. The hair was often draped quite low over the forehead, sometimes nearly touching the eyebrows.

Figure 6.4   In this picture, notice that the ears are covered, the wavy hair is draped low across the forehead, and the bulk of the hair has been piled on the back of the head.

The Orientalism trend (popularized by designers like Paul Poiret) also led to a craze for turbans. These turbans sometimes made a narrower hairstyle necessary, so that the hair would fit inside the turban. The large picture hats that were still in fashion required the support of a larger, wider hairstyle. Your fashion preferences would definitely have influenced your hairstyle during this era! In addition to turbans, fabric bandeaus and jeweled headpieces were often worn in this period, giving the hairstyles a vaguely Grecian look. Examples of this trend can be seen in Figures 6.1 and 6.5.

Figure 6.5   A woman wears a jeweled headband, a style that was popular in the teens.

At this time in history, Madame C.J. Walker was pioneering the development of hair care products for African-Americans. Suffragettes begin to make simpler hairstyle choices to complement more masculinely tailored clothes. Movies also begin to influence fashion. Late in the decade, dancer Irene Castle begins to make short hair popular, a trend that would explode in popularity in the 1920s.

Figure 6.6 An example of the shorter hairstyle that was popular in the latter half of the decade between 1910 and 1920.

Men in the Teens

Men's hair in the Teens continued to be simple, short, and neat. The hair was often slicked straight back off of the head, although styles with a part could still be found.

Figure 6.7 Members of the Louisiana Five jazz band looking over papers. Left to right: Anton Lada, Charles Panely, Alcide Nunez, Karl Berger, Joe Cawley. Date: 1919. Courtesy of Nunez family collection. These band members wear a variety of slicked back hairstyles.

The hair was often cropped so short that the skin was visible through the hair over the ears.

Figure 6.8 Wallace Beery, circa 1914 in Chicago, wears his hair cut extremely short over the ears.

The occasional neatly groomed mustache could still be found during this period, but the trend was generally toward being clean shaven.

Teens Woman's Styling—Step by Step Instructions

This hairstyle was inspired by Figure 6.4, but with a narrower silhouette.

Figure 6.9   Step 1. Begin with a wig that is very long (at least 16 inches at the nape of the neck) and mostly one length. You may also need to incorporate a matching color switch in the final hairstyle. For this style, I used a synthetic lace front wig and a matching switch.

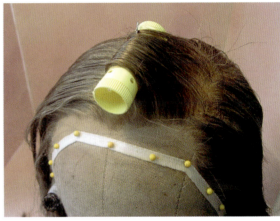

Figure 6.10   Step 2. Make a side part in the wig, and begin setting a dime-sized roller to one side of the part.

Figure 6.11   Step 3. Continue setting the rollers horizontally down the side of the head. Increase to quarter-sized rollers once you get to the temple area. As you set the rollers, pull the hair slightly down onto the forehead.

Figure 6.12   Step 4. On the other side of the part, you can set a tendril of hair on a dime-sized roller if there happen to be short layers in your wig. Set a row of horizontal rollers going down the side of the head, just as you did on the opposite side. The first roller beside the part should be angled slightly so that it forms a V shape with the roller on the other side of the part. Again, move from dime-sized rollers to quarter-sized rollers.

Figure 6.13   Step 5. Set a dime-sized roller directly behind the V of the rollers at the part. Use quarter-sized rollers to set alternating diagonal rows back to the crown of the head.

Figure 6.14   Step 6. Just below the crown of the head, pull a section of hair into a small ponytail.

Figure 6.15   Step 7. Set the hair in the ponytail onto several dime-sized rollers.

Figure 6.16   Step 8. Use quarter-sized rollers to set the hair below the ponytail rolling towards the ponytail. If there are any shorter tendrils of hair behind the ears, set them on pencil-sized rollers.

Figure 6.17   Step 9. The finished set at the nape of the neck.

Teens Woman's Hairstyle—The Finished Set

Figures 6.18–21   The finished Teens Woman's style set.

Once you have finished setting the wig, steam each roller thoroughly if the wig is made of synthetic hair. If the wig is human hair, soak each roller with water sprayed from a spray bottle. After steaming or wetting, place the wig in a wig dryer for 75 minutes.

To style:

Figure 6.22 Step 10. Remove all of the rollers from the wig, beginning at the nape of the neck. Brush through the entire wig with a large brush.

Figure 6.23 Step 11. Lightly tease the hair all around the hairline.

Figure 6.24 Step 12. Use a teasing/smoothing brush to smooth the teased hair down and away from the part. Make sure to brush the hair down onto the forehead.

Figure 6.25 Step 13. Use the brush to make sure that there is a clear divide between the front section that is smoothed towards the ears, and the back section that is smoothed towards the crown of the head.

Figure 6.26 Step 14. Use a piece of blocking tape to shape the hair in the front section into large waves.

Figure 6.27 Step 15. On the other side of the head, pull the front section back over the ear and twist it a little bit. Pin the twist in place.

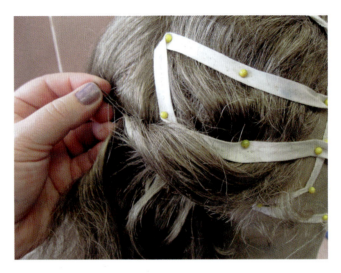

Figure 6.28   Step 16. Pull the hair at the bottom of the waved section up and twist it and pin it like you did on the other side.

Figure 6.29   Step 17. Pin a hair pad in a matching color just above the small ponytail you created earlier. Notice how the remaining hair in the front section has been pinned up out of the way with a duckbill clip.

Figure 6.30   Step 18. Pull the hair in the ponytail up over the hair pad and anchor it with crossed bobby pins. It is not necessary for the entire hair pad to be covered at this time, as you are going to dress more hair over it in later steps.

Figure 6.31   Step 19. Divide the bottom section of the wig in half. Lightly tease the left side of the wig and mist it with hairspray.

Figure 6.32   Step 20. Smooth this left section diagonally up the back of the wig and pin it so that the section covers the outside part of the hair pad.

Figure 6.33   Step 21. Tease and smooth the right side of the wig diagonally up and over towards the left side of the hair pad (it should overlap the first section you did). Pin this section in place.

Figure 6.34   Step 22. Begin arranging the loose hair at the ends of the sections into curls and rolls by brushing sections of hair around your finger with a smoothing brush.

Figure 6.35   Step 23. Arrange the rest of the hair into loops and rolls around the hair pad. You may need to move and pin sections of hair around in order to create a balanced final product.

Figure 6.36   Step 24. Once you have arranged all of the hair, cover it with a matching color hairnet and pin so that the hairnet does not show.

Figure 6.37   Step 25. You could finish the hairstyle at this point, and dress it with a bandeau or headband.

Figure 6.38   Step 26. If you wish to create a fuller, more elaborate hairstyle, pin a matching switch underneath the center of the finished curl cluster.

Figure 6.39   Step 27. I created the texture in this switch by simply braiding it and setting it. Once dry, I unbraided the switch and used the wavy texture as part of the finished look. Wrap the switch up and around the cluster of curls. Pin the hair in place with hairpins as you move around the head.

Figure 6.40   Step 28. Hide the tail end of your switch under the bottom of your curl cluster. Pin it in place with bobby pins.

Teens Woman—The Completed Hairstyle

Figures 6.41–44 The completed Teens Woman's style. Photography: Tim Babiak. Model: Josephine McAdam.

Variations

Varying the placement of the fullness in the hairstyle will allow you to create many different Teens-appropriate looks. You can also include the occasional shorter hairstyle, such as the one in Figure 6.6. Another hairstyle variety you can use is to pile the hair on top of the head and secure the bulk of it with a bandeau, and let the ends of the hair hang down by the ears, such as in Figure 6.45. This gives the illusion of a shorter hairstyle while still maintaining the fullness typical of hairstyles of this period.

Figure 6.45   This portrait gives the impression of a bobbed hairstyle while still maintaining the length of the hair.

seven

THE 1920S

{ *1920–1929* }

Figure 7.1   Advertisement for mannequins by Pierre Imans, c.1925–30 (colour litho), French School, (20th century) / Private Collection / Archives Charmet / The Bridgeman Art Library International.

1920s Women

Fashion changed dramatically for women in the 1920s. After hundreds of years of being confined in corsets and having long hair put up into elaborate hairstyles, women gained new freedom from their clothes and heavy hair.

Beginning in World War 1, nearly all of the women who drove ambulances had their hair cut for reasons of sanitation and ease. In popular culture, a ballroom dancer by the name of Irene Castle cut off her long hair for reasons of convenience. The trend spread rapidly, and women everywhere began bobbing their hair.

Important Events

1920	Prohibition begins
1920	The Nineteenth Amendment, giving women the right to vote, is ratified in the United States
1922	The tomb of King Tut is discovered in Egypt
1927	*The Jazz Singer*, the first feature length movie with recorded dialogue, debuts
1928	Mickey Mouse debuts in the animated short "Steamboat Willie"
1929	Several gangsters are shot and killed in the St. Valentine's Day Massacre
1929	The stock market crashes, beginning the Great Depression

Important Artists/Designers

Coco Chanel, Erté, Max Factor, Salvatore Ferragamo, Jeanne Lanvin, Tamara de Lempicka, Maxfield Parrish, Jean Patou, Man Ray, Elsa Schiaparelli.

Important People/Style Icons

Josephine Baker, Theda Bara, John Barrymore, Clara Bow, Louise Brooks, Al Capone, Charlie Chaplin, F. Scott and Zelda Fitzgerald, Ernest Hemingway, Al Jolson, Buster Keaton, Charles Lindbergh, Gloria Swanson, Rudolph Valentino.

Figure 7.2 This woman models a typical bobbed haircut of the 1920s.

In May of 1920, the *Saturday Evening Post* published F. Scott Fitzgerald's short story "Bernice Bobs Her Hair." This story of a small town girl who is tricked by her cousin into chopping off her hair and subsequently becomes a *femme fatale* further served to give this haircut a special place in history. Fashion was also undergoing a revolution—women's clothes were less confining, and more masculine shapes were very much in vogue. The close fitting cloche hats of the era also required short simple haircuts to fit underneath. An example of a 1920s hat can he seenin Figure 7.3

Figure 7.3 A woman models a close fitting cloche hat that covers nearly all of her short cropped haircut.

There were many variations of the bob haircut. The Shingle involved cutting the hair close to the scalp at the nape of the neck and leaving the hair gradually longer as the barber went higher, without showing a definite line. This haircut was very easy to style in a number of ways. The Eton Crop was a very short haircut, named after the English boy's public school, that left both the ears and neck exposed. This haircut was made popular by Josephine Baker (Figure 7.4), the famous African-American entertainer who rose to fame performing in France.

Figure 7.4 Josephine Baker (1906–75) (b/w photo), French Photographer (20th century) / Private Collection / Archives Charmet / The Bridgeman Art Library International. Josephine Baker and her short, pomaded hairstyle.

The Dutch Boy bob was made famous by movie stars Louise Brooks and Colleen Moore. This haircut was usually worn straight to just above the jaw line, with blunt cut bangs helping to frame the face.

Figure 7.5   Louise Brooks models her iconic Dutch Boy bob haircut.

Another film star who set trends in the 1920s was Clara Bow. Her tousled curls, sad, down-turned eyes, and well defined cupid's bow lip earned her the nickname of the "It Girl."

Figure 7.6   Clara Bow's curls are an example of a 1920s hairstyle with a lot of texture.

In the earlier part of the 1920s, hair was often shorter, smoother, and sleeker, such as in Figures 7.2, 7.5, and 7.7. This texture was often achieved by water waving or finger waving, a method of hair dressing that involved wetting the hair with curling lotion, combing it into waves with your fingers, and letting it dry.

Figure 7.7   A short, simple hairstyle, typical of the early part of the 1920s.

Later in the decade, hairstyles had more texture—either like the messy curls of Clara Bow, or the more rigidly defined waves seen in Figure 7.8. The more rigid styles were likely created with a Marcel curling iron, an iron that created a three dimensional wave when pressed into the hair.

to wear a romantic style of hair with long ringlets, made popular by silent actress Mary Pickford, who was famous for playing plucky young *ingénues*. Whether women's hair was long or bobbed, the silhouette was very close to the head, and the hair was usually dressed low on the forehead.

Figure 7.8   A more textured hairstyle, typical of the later part of the 1920s.

Despite the prevalence of the bob, some women refused to believe the trend would last. They feared cutting their hair, only to literally come up short when long hair came back into fashion. Many of these women secured their hair in a tight low bun that mimicked the close fitting silhouette of the bob. Other women chose

Figure 7.9   A woman wearing a version of the long romantic ringlets that were popular in the 1920s. Also note how her hair is dressed low across her forehead.

1920s Men

Men in the 1920s often had haircuts where the hair was longer on the top and sides, but quite short and neatly trimmed in the back. Like the women of the period, men also had Marcel waves in their hair. Movie stars like Rudolph Valentino helped set the fashion of heavily slicked back hair.

Figure 7.10   Movie star Rudolph Valentino's slicked back hair and heavily made up face were a popular look in the 1920s.

Men following this fashion were often referred to as "sheiks"—this term came from the characters in all of the Arabian/Middle Eastern film settings popular at the time. To achieve the desired slicked back, cleanly parted looks, men used hair products like brilliantine, an oily grooming liquid for hair that gave a highly glossy finish. Brylcreem also made its debut in this decade—it was invented as a pomade in England in 1928.

Not all men adopted the slicked back look. Some men wore their hair in a looser, more adventurous looking textured hairstyle, such as the look worn by Charles Lindbergh.

Figure 7.11   Charles Lindbergh, with his plane The Spirit of St. Louis, in 1927.

Stylish mustaches were very fashionable in the 1920s. Because women were enjoying freedom through short boyish haircuts and more masculine clothing, men would grow mustaches to assert their masculinity. Popular styles of mustache included the very thin pencil mustache and the short toothbrush mustache popularized by Charlie Chaplin (Figure 7.12).

Figure 7.12   Charlie Chaplin with Jackie Coogan in a still from the 1921 movie *"The Kid"*.

1920s Flapper Styling—Step by Step Instructions

This hairstyle was inspired by Figure 7.2, with a little more curl added for visual definition.

Figure 7.13   Step 1. Begin with a wig that is cut quite short in the back, with longer hair (at least 4 inches long) on the top, front, and sides. (This wig could actually be used without any additional styling as another kind of 1920s look—it resembles the styles in Figures 7.5 and 7.7.) I used a fully ventilated lace front human hair wig for this styling project.

Figure 7.14   Step 2. Make a clean part in the wig. Comb setting lotion through the wig.

Figure 7.15   Step 3. Use a rat tail comb to section out an area of hair that is approximately 1 inch by 1 inch square.

Figure 7.16   Step 4. Use a dowel rod to roll the section of hair into a pin curl.

Figure 7.17 Step 5. This curl is rolled clockwise towards the face, coming forward of the hairline.

Figure 7.18 Step 6. Continue rolling pin curls in a horizontal row around the head. All of the curls in this row should be rolled clockwise.

Figure 7.19 Step 7. As you come around the part, continue rolling the curls in a clockwise direction.

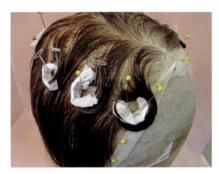

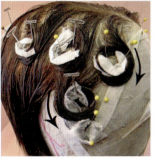

Figure 7.20 Step 8. The last pin curl in this row should also come forward of the hairline. Setting your curls in front of the hairline is especially helpful if you are styling a hard front wig—this will help the waves conceal the edge of the wig once the hair is styled.

Figure 7.21 Step 9. The next row of pin curls should be rolled in a counterclockwise direction. Also make a tiny pin curl in front of the ear.

Figure 7.22 Step 10. Continue rolling the pin curls counterclockwise in a horizontal row.

Figure 7.23 Step 11. Finish this row of pin curls with a curl that comes past the hairline onto the face. Make another small pin curl in front of the ear. If there is enough length in the hair, make a small pin curl behind the ear.

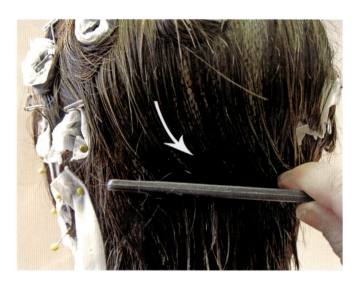

Figure 7.24 Step 12. The rest of the hair in this wig is too short to pin curl. (If the hair in your wig is long enough, continue pin curling the wig all the way down to the nape of the neck in alternating rows.) Instead, we are going to finger wave the back. Begin by combing all of the hair to the right. You may need to add more setting lotion and water if the wig has become too dry.

Figure 7.25 Step 13. Secure the hair in this direction by pinning a piece of blocking tape over it.

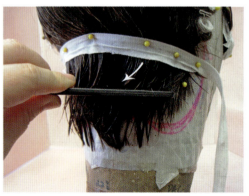

Figure 7.26 Step 14. Drop down and comb the hair back to the left. Secure it in place with the blocking tape.

Figure 7.27 Step 15. Finish off the set by combing the ends of the hair back towards the right and securing them with the tape.

1920s Flapper—The Final Set

Figures 7.28–31 The finished 1920s Flapper style set.

Once you have finished setting the wig, steam it if the wig is made of synthetic hair. If the wig is made of human hair (as this one is) spray it liberally with water. Put the wig in a wig dryer to dry for 75 minutes.

To style the wig:

Figure 7.32   Step 16. Remove the blocking tape from the back of the wig and undo all of the pin curls, removing the end papers.

Figure 7.33   Step 17. Use a wide toothed comb to comb through all of the pin curls.

Figure 7.34   Step 18. The wig after it has been completely combed through.

Figure 7.35   Step 19. Use a rat tail comb to comb through the wig even more finely.

Figure 7.36   Step 20. Use the end of the rat tail comb to section out the hair next to the part.

Figure 7.37   Step 21. Use a teasing/smoothing brush to lightly tease the underside of the hair in the section.

Figure 7.38 Step 22. After teasing the hair, use the brush to smooth the hair back down. Next, use the brush to brush the curls at the ends of the hair around your fingers to make them neat.

Figure 7.39 Step 23. After you have formed the curls around your finger, gently pull them apart and arrange them in an attractive way. Continue smoothing and arranging the curls, working your way around the entire head.

Figure 7.40 Step 24. Once you have finished the curls, use a piece of blocking tape to hold the waves in place.

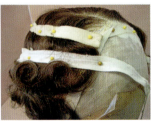

Figure 7.41 Step 25. Use the tape to pull the wave onto the forehead.

Figures 7.42 and 7.43 Step 26. Continue pinning the waves and curls in place with the blocking tape.

Figure 7.44 Step 27. You can also arrange the curls where you want them by holding them in place with pins. Once you have finished taping and pinning the hair, mist the wig with hairspray and let it set overnight. When you are ready to use the wig, carefully unpin and remove the blocking tape and pins.

1920s Flapper—The Completed Style

Figures 7.45–48   The completed 1920s Flapper style. Photography: Tim Babiak. Model: Ivy Negron.

Variations

1920s looks were usually dark, dramatic, and exotic. You can vary the looks by mixing in a range of dark colors, from jet black to deep auburn. You can purchase Dutch Boy bob wigs that are ready to go straight out of the box. You can also purchase short boyish straight wigs and short waved wigs that do not require much styling that are appropriate to this period.

You can also create sleek, finger waved looks à la Josephine Baker. To do this, use a short wig. Comb a generous amount of setting lotion throughout the entire wig. Use blocking tapes to create sculpted waves, working back and forth around the head.

Figures 7.49–52 The finished sleek finger wave set, created with blocking tape and pins setting the waves, and curl clips setting the pin curls.

Sleek 1920s Look—The Completed Style

Figures 7.53–56 The sleek 1920s look, styled by Maur Sela. Photography: Tim Babiak. Model: Ivy Negron.

eight

THE 1930S

{ *1930–1939* }

Figure 8.1 Still from the film "Shanghai Express" with Marlene Dietrich and Clive Brook, 1932 (photo), German photographer (20th Century) / Private Collection / The Bridgeman Art Library International.

Important Events

1931	The Empire State Building is completed.
1932	Amelia Earhart flies solo across the Atlantic Ocean
1932	The Lindbergh baby (son of Charles Lindbergh) is kidnapped
1933	Prohibition ends in the United States
1936	King Edward VIII abdicates the British throne in order to marry Wallis Simpson
1937	Amelia Earhart vanishes
1937	The Hindenburg blimp explodes
1939	World War II begins

Important Artists/Designers

Grant Wood, Mark Rothko, Salvador Dalí, Adrian, Madame Grès, Madeleine Vionnet.

Important People/Style Icons

Joan Crawford, Bette Davis, Marlene Dietrich, Douglas Fairbanks, Jr., Errol Flynn, Clark Gable, Greta Garbo, Jean Harlow, Lana Turner, Mae West, Anna Mae Wong.

1930s Women

The 1930s took the radical new looks of the 1920s and intensified them, making them even more glamorous and detailed. Hairstyles moved away from the more boyish looks of the 1920s towards a more voluptuous and feminine look. For example, in Figure 8.2, Mae West's hairstyle displays the more exaggerated sculptural waves that define this period.

Figure 8.2 Movie star Mae West's hair shows both the voluptuous waves and the platinum blonde color that helped define the 1930s.

Hats also remained a hugely important fashion element in the 1930s. The hats of this era moved from the cloche hats of the 1920s that covered nearly the entire head to smaller hats that perched on the head like a plate, often at a jaunty angle. This led to many 1930s hairstyles being rather smooth on top, such as in the hairstyle on Bette Davis in Figure 8.3.

Figure 8.3 Bette Davis's hairstyle is an example of a 1930s hairstyle that is smoother on top.

Figure 8.4 Jean Harlow, the original 1930s blonde bombshell.

beauty of stars like Shearer and Greta Garbo. This wave would dip further and further down onto the face until it became the peek-a-boo look that was popular in the 1940s.

Even if the hairstyle was smoother on top, there were usually still small curls framing the face. Hair during this period was often set using either pin curls, finger waves, or a combination of both. Setting lotions or curling fluid helped provide the sleek control often seen in styles from this era. The 1930s was also the era of the peroxide blonde. Film star Jean Harlow (Figure 8.4) caused a stir when she bleached her hair to a platinum blonde color for the film *Platinum Blonde*.

Another movie star look that was popular in the 1930s was a deep side part with a wave that dipped down on the opposite side of the face, such as the one shown on Norma Shearer (Figure 8.5). This wave accentuated the mysterious

Figure 8.5 Norma Shearer models a hairstyle with a deep, defined side part and waves dipping down onto her forehead.

1930s Men

The ideal gentleman in the 1930s was clean cut, with neatly trimmed, groomed, and pomaded hair, and a clean shaven face, such as in the advertisement in Figure 8.6. Matinée idols, as in the 1920s, continued to set the trends for audiences everywhere. The exaggerated slicked back hair and heavily made up face of the 1920s gave way to a more realistic looking man in the 1930s. The hair was still controlled with pomades and other products, but the finish was not as glassy as the previous decade. No facial hair at all was the dominant trend, but several prominent actors, including Clark Gable (Figure 8.7) and Errol Flynn (Figure 8.8) sported a neat, well groomed pencil mustache.

Figure 8.7 Movie star Clark Gable without his trademark mustache. His neatly parted, well groomed hair is very typical of the 1930s.

Figure 8.8 Errol Flynn's pencil mustache added to his dashing air that personified his adventurous movie roles.

1930s Blonde Bombshell Styling— Step by Step Instructions

The reference picture for this hairstyle is Figure 8.1, worn by Marlene Dietrich.

Figure 8.9   Step 1. Begin with a wig that is just below chin length, with layers of 4–6 inch long hair throughout the wig. I used a platinum blonde lace front wig made with synthetic hair.

Figure 8.10   Step 2. Use a small dowel rod to set a tiny pin curl in front of each ear. Secure the pin curl with roundhead pins.

Figure 8.11   Step 3. Make a side part in the hair. I have chosen to place the part on the left side for this style. Comb a small amount of setting lotion mixed with water throughout the wig. Because the wig in the example is synthetic, large amounts of setting lotion are not needed to shape the style, because steaming the set will also help hold the set. Once you have distributed the product through the wig, comb the hair at the part away from the face.

Figure 8.12   Step 4. Use a larger dowel rod (approximately the diameter of a quarter) to begin shaping your pin curls. This first row of pin curls should be rolled in a counterclockwise direction.

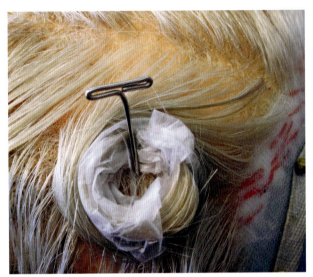

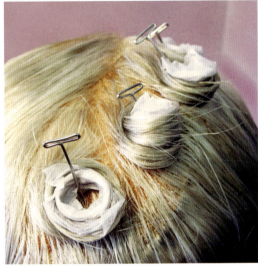

Figure 8.13   Step 5. Secure the finished pin curl with a curl clip, hairpin, or t-pin (shown here).

Figure 8.14   Step 6. Work your way along the part, rolling all of your pin curls in the same direction (counterclockwise).

Figure 8.15   Step 7. Continue setting the hair in counterclockwise pin curls as you circle around the part. Comb the hair on the other side of the part towards the face.

Figure 8.16   Step 8. Continue rolling the pin curls in a counter clockwise direction. As you get to the hairline of the wig, allow the pin curl to dip down onto the forehead. A small round head pin has been used here to provide a little lift to the hair right at the part.

Figure 8.17   Step 9. The finished first row of pin curls, viewed from the top.

Figure 8.18   Step 10. The next row of pin curls will be rolled in a clockwise direction. Begin by combing the next section of hair away from the face.

Figure 8.19   Step 11. Roll the first pin curl of the second curl so that it sits slightly behind the hairline. Continue rolling the pin curls in this row clockwise, working your way around the head.

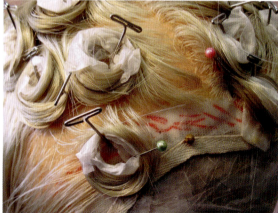

Figure 8.20   Step 12. When you get to the last pin curl of this row, set that curl so that it comes onto the face, past the hairline. Setting curls in front of the hairline is very helpful when you are styling a hard front wig—it will help you conceal the front edge of the wig.

Figure 8.21   Step 13. The completed second row of pin curls, viewed from the top.

Figure 8.22   Step 14. The third row of pin curls should be rolled counterclockwise (in the same direction as the first row). However, because the hairstyle we are creating is asymmetrical, the third row of pin curls should only go about halfway around the head.

Figure 8.23   Step 15. The remaining hair on the left side of the wig should be set with a small roller.

Figure 8.24   Step 16. Go back to the right side of the wig. Comb the hair towards the face.

Figure 8.25   Step 17. Begin rolling the hair on dime-sized rollers. The rollers should be rolled toward the face and be placed diagonally.

Figure 8.26   Step 18. Continue rolling diagonal sections of hair, working your way around the wig. The last roller should meet up with the first roller you placed on the left side of the wig.

Figure 8.27   Step 19. The next row of rollers should also be set in diagonal sections, but this time, the diagonal is going away from the face on this side (when you reach the opposite side, it will be going away from the face).

Figure 8.28   Step 20. As you work your way down the wig, keep alternating the direction of your diagonal sections. You will also likely need to use smaller rollers as you get to the shorter layers of hair at the bottom of the wig.

1930s Blonde Bombshell—The Finished Set

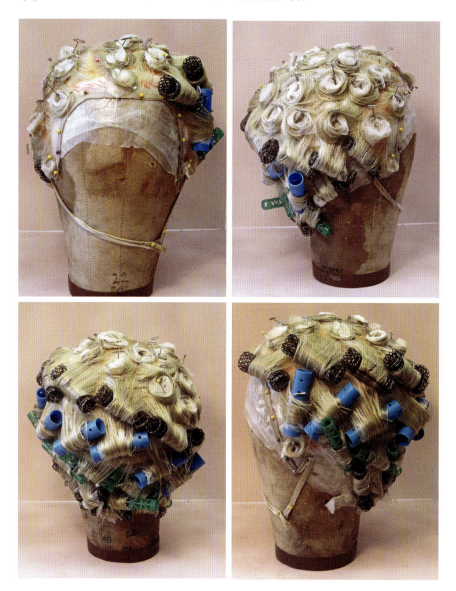

Figures 8.29–32 The completed 1930s set, viewed from all angles.

The set is now complete. If the wig is synthetic hair, steam the set in place. If the wig is human hair, thoroughly wet the finished set. Place the wig in a wig dryer for 75 minutes.

Once the wig is completely dry and cool, it is time to style it.

Figure 8.33 Step 21. Begin removing the rollers at the nape of the neck of the wig and work your way up until all of the rollers have been removed. Do not undo the pin curls yet.

Figure 8.34 Step 22. As you unroll each row of rollers, use a wide toothed comb to gently pick through the curls.

Figure 8.35 Step 23. Continue to use the pick to comb out all of the unrolled hair. Once you have completed the combing, go ahead and undo the pin curls.

Figure 8.36 Step 24. Use a smoothing brush to thoroughly brush through the hair that was set in pin curls.

Figure 8.37 Step 25. After brushing through the section, use your hand to pat the hair towards the part until the waves begin falling into place.

Figure 8.38 Step 26. Use a long piece of blocking tape to block the waves in place. Pin the blocking tape in the center of the crest of the first wave. Pin every inch or so to hold the wave in place. Make sure to close all gaps and breaks in the waves as you are pinning the blocking tape.

Figure 8.39 Step 27. Work your way, back and forth around the head, just as you did when you were setting the pin curls. Here is a top view of the blocking tape being pinned into place.

Figure 8.40 Step 28. Use the tape to push the ridges of the waves up so that they are more defined.

Figure 8.41   Step 29. All of the wavy section has now been taped and pinned in place.

Figure 8.42   Step 30. Notice how the pinned waves do not go all the way around on the right side of the wig. This is because the hairstyle is asymmetrical.

Figure 8.43   Step 31. Use a lifting comb to fluff out the curls on the rest of the wig.

Figure 8.44   Step 32. Use a rat tail comb to shape each curl around your finger until you are happy with the placement of each. Once you have made all of the wig's curls neat, spray the wig with hairspray.

Figure 8.45   Step 33. Allow the wig to sit at least overnight so that the waves and curls may settle into place. Once you are ready to use the wig, remove the tapes and unpin the wig from the canvas block.

1930s Blonde Bombshell—The Completed Hairstyle

Figures 8.46–49   The completed 1930s Blonde Bombshell style. Photography: Tim Babiak. Model: Ariel Livingston.

Variations

You can achieve variety in your 1930s wig looks by changing the location of the part. You can also experiment with texture. Smoothing each curl around your finger may create an elegant screen siren; picking out those curls so that they have a frizzy texture may look more like a ditzy showgirl. Some styles remained sleeker—you could use the blocking tape to secure the waves all the way down and eliminate the curled section entirely. You could use a larger dowel rod to create bigger pin curls on the top section—this will make the top smoother, like the style seen in the photograph of Bette Davis (Figure 8.3). While the platinum blondes dominated the trends, there were still darker mysterious beauties like Greta Garbo, so do not be afraid to use a variety of hair colors.

Figures 8.50 and 8.51   Anna Fugate's wig style is one that is much smoother on the top, with defined curls in the back.

nine

THE 1940S

{ *1940–1949* }

Figure 9.1   Catchy Number, c.1946 (colour litho), American School (probably Gil Elvgren) (20th century) / Private Collection / DaTo Images / The Bridgeman Art Library International.

Important Events

Important Artists/ Designers

Cristobal Balenciaga, Gil Elvgren, Willem de Kooning, Edward Hopper, Jeanne Lanvin, Jean Patou, Jackson Pollock, Mark Rothko, Elsa Schiaparelli, Alberto Vargas, Andrew Wyeth.

Important People/Style Icons

Lauren Bacall, Humphrey Bogart, Ava Gardner, Rita Hayworth, Lena Horne, Veronica Lake, Hedy Lamarr, Carmen Miranda, Rosalind Russell, Lana Turner, Esther Williams.

1940s Women

The 1940s was the decade of pinup models, sweater girls, and back home sweethearts. As World War II raged on in Europe, women back home often went to work and took on traditionally masculine jobs that were left empty when thousands of soldiers went to war. Ironically, although gender roles were changing, women's fashion was becoming extremely feminine. Hairstyles were growing longer—the 1920s bob became the 1930s shingle, which then became the 1940s pageboy.

Figure 9.2   A studio promotional photo of actress Lauren Bacall showing a typical version of the 1940s pageboy hairstyle.

This longer, more feminine haircut provided many style options, and popular movie actresses were still setting the trends in hair. Movies were thought to keep up spirits during wartime, and thus they dominated popular entertainment in the 1940s. Movie magazine and cosmetics ads (such as the one in Figure 9.3) made it even easier for the average woman to access all the details of her favorite star's look.

Figure 9.3 Esther Williams (b.1923) advertising "Max Factor" cosmetics, from *"Marie-France"* magazine, October 1947 (colour litho), French School (20th century) / Bibliothèque des Arts Decoratifs, Paris, France / Archives Charmet / The Bridgeman Art Library International.

Actress Veronica Lake was famous for her long blonde peek-a-boo hairstyle that mysteriously draped over one eye.

Figure 9.4 Veronica Lake's signature wavy hairstyle.

Rita Hayworth wore a similar hairstyle dyed red. These long hairstyles were eventually thought to be a danger to women working in factories. Veronica Lake actually changed her widely imitated hairstyle to encourage factory safety. One method women used to keep their long hair from catching in machinery was putting it up in a snood, as seen in Figure 9.5.

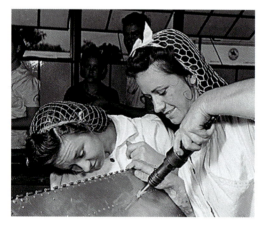

Figure 9.5 Detail from *Women Workers*, 1942 "Two sisters who left the farm to keep our airmen flying. NYA trainees at the Corpus Christi, Texas Naval Air Base, Evelyn and Lillian Buxkeurple are shown working on a practice bombshell." Source: Franklin D. Roosevelt Library and Museum.

This style soon took on such popularity that the women began wearing it outside the factories. Head scarves and bandannas, like the one worn by Rosie the Riveter, were also used to tie hair up out of the way. Also gaining in fashion trends was the elaborate updo. These hairstyles took the trend of wearing hair neatly back in a snood and took it one step further. All of the hair was swept off of the neck and piled on top of the head in elaborate curls. Bangs helped to keep this style feminine. The bangs might be worn in a thick wave (Figure 9.6) or in a cluster of curls (Figure 9.7).

Figure 9.6   The hairstyle how-to illustration shows off Alexis Smith's thick wavy bangs and tightly rolled "Victory rolls" in the back.

Figure 9.7   Famous pinup girl Betty Grable's hairstyle features tightly curled bangs.

1940s Men

Men's hairstyle trends in the 1940s were usually determined by one of two things: movie stars or the military. Many men were forced to obey military regulations for their hair. These hairstyles were very short, buzzed almost to the skin in the back, and trimmed high over the ears. Some versions, like the high and tight haircut, left the hair slightly longer on top of the head. Crew cuts and flattops were also becoming popular haircuts at this time.

Figure 9.8   1940s bandleader Glenn Miller wears a short, military haircut.

One extremely popular version of the updo was Victory rolls. These sculptural rolls of hair are what many people think of when they think of 1940s hair. True Victory rolls roll all the way down the head, forming a "V" shape in back (much like those in Figure 9.6). There is also a version of the hairstyle where just the hair around the face is rolled and the length of the hair is left loose in the back.

Civilian men, like military men, wore the back and sides of their haircuts very short and neat. The lines around the ears and neck were sharp and very precise. The hair on the top of the head was left longer. It might be parted on the side, or combed straight back—both ways used products like Brylcreem to hold the style in place. Natural wave to the hair was very fashionable, and the hairstyles were combed in such a way as to accentuate the waves of the hair in front.

Figures 9.9 and 9.10 Both Cary Grant (left) and Mario Lanza (right) wore versions of a slicked back hairstyle with the waves in the front accentuated.

1940s Glamour Girl/Peek-a-Boo Styling—Step by Step Instructions

This hairstyle was inspired by the photograph of Veronica Lake, seen in Figure 9.4.

Figure 9.11 Step 1. Begin with a wig that is at least shoulder length (8–12 inches long at the nape of the neck is ideal). Long layers around the face are also helpful in creating this hairstyle. I used a fully ventilated lace front human hair wig that is in the longer range for this hairstyle.

Figure 9.12 Step 2. Thoroughly wet the hair with water and setting lotion. Make a deep side part in the wig with the end of your rat tail comb. Comb the hair above the part away from the face.

Figure 9.13 Step 3. Separate out a section of hair that is approximately 1 inch by 1 inch square. Use a dowel rod to make a pin curl in the wig, winding the hair clockwise towards the face.

Figure 9.14 Step 4. After sliding the hair off of the dowel rod, give the pin curl a slight push towards the part. This will give lift to the root of the hair in the pin curl.

Figure 9.15 Step 5. Use t-pins, curl clips, or hairpins to secure the pin curl in place.

Figure 9.16 Step 6. Make a second pin curl behind the first one, still rolling the hair away from the face in a clockwise direction. Continue working your way around the part, setting pin curls.

Figure 9.17 Step 7. As you come around the part, continue combing the hair in the same direction. The hair below the part will now be combed going towards the face.

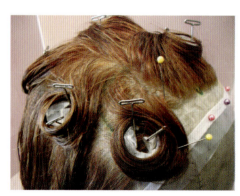

Figure 9.18 Step 8. The last pin curl should break the hairline and come forward onto the face.

Figure 9.19   Step 9. For the next row, roll the hair going towards the face on a nickel-sized roller. Pin the roller so that it sits vertically.

Figure 9.20   Step 10. Continue setting nickel-sized rollers around the back of the head. These rollers should sit diagonally.

Figure 9.21   Step 11. As you work your way around the head, the rollers will sit higher up on the head. The last roller should sit just in front of the hairline. I have also placed a round headed pin in to give a bit of extra lift at the hairline.

Figure 9.22   Step 12. Drop down another row and set this roller going towards the face.

Figures 9.23 and 9.24   Step 13. This next row of rollers should be set in the opposite diagonal direction from the row above. Finish this row with a dime-sized roller (the yellow roller in Figure 9.24).

Figure 9.25   Step 14. The next row of rollers below should again change direction, beginning with a dime-sized roller rolled towards the face.

Figure 9.26   Step 15. Continue setting this row of rollers around the head. Alternate diagonal rows of rollers until you reach the bottom of the wig. I used pencil-sized rollers at the bottom of the wig in order to get a tighter curl.

1940s Glamour Girl—The Finished Set

Figures 9.27–30 The finished Glamour Girl/Peek-a Boo style set.

Once you have finished setting the wig, steam each roller thoroughly if the wig is made of synthetic hair. If the wig is human hair, soak each roller with water sprayed from a spray bottle. After steaming or wetting, place the wig in a wig dryer for seventy-five minutes.

To style:

Figure 9.31   Step 16. Begin removing the rollers from the bottom of the wig, working your way up to the top.

Figure 9.32   Step 17. The wig with all of the rollers and pin curls removed.

Figure 9.33   Step 18. Use a large brush to completely brush through the entire wig.

Figure 9.34   Step 19. Once the wig is brushed out, it will appear very soft. The shape of the waves should begin to be visible.

Figure 9.35 Step 20. Lightly tease the underside of the hair on the top of the wig. This will add a little volume to the wig and smooth out any roller breaks.

Figure 9.36 Step 21. Use your teasing/smoothing brush to smooth the hair in the top section back into place. Use your fingers to push the hair and help define the shape of the wave.

Figure 9.37 Step 22. Pin a piece of blocking tape in place and use it to hold and define the shape of the waves.

Figure 9.38 Step 23. Continue pinning the tape around the part until you come around the other side. Use the tape to shape the wave onto the face.

Figure 9.39 Step 24. Work your way back around the head, following the shape of the waves.

Figure 9.40 Step 25. The wave on the opposite side of the face should now also come forward of the hairline.

Figure 9.41   Step 26. Brush the hair below the part around your finger with your smoothing brush. This will create a nice sculpted curl that finishes off that side of the hairstyle.

Figure 9.42   Step 27. Pin another piece of tape next to the curl you just created, and use it to define the waves under the curve of the head.

Figure 9.43   Step 28. Gather the remaining hair into your hand and brush it around a finger or two, shaping the hair into a large curl.

Figure 9.44   Step 29. Smoothly roll this curl underneath, shaping it with your fingers.

Figures 9.45 and 9.46   Step 30. Place a large hairnet over the back of the wig and use it to sculpt the hair into shape. Pin the hairnet until you are pleased with the way the hair is placed in the back. Mist the wig with hairspray and let it sit until the wig is ready to be worn.

1940s Glamour Girl—The Completed Hairstyle

Figures 9.47–50 The completed Glamour Girl/Peek-a-Boo style. Photography: Tim Babiak. Model: Sabrina Lotfi.

1940s Pinup Girl/Victory Rolls Styling— Step by Step Instructions

This hairstyle combines elements of Figures 9.6 and 9.7, with more defined rolls at the front of the wig.

Figure 9.51   Step 1. Again, begin with a wig that at least comes to the shoulders (8–12 inches from the nape of the neck). I used a fully ventilated human hair lace front wig.

Figure 9.52   Step 2. Use your rat tail comb to make a clean center part in the wig.

Figure 9.53   Step 3. Beginning at one side of the center part, set two nickel-sized rollers rolling away from the part. Set two more rollers angling down and back from the temple area. Repeat on the other side of the wig.

Figure 9.54   Step 4. Behind the center part, set a nickel-sized roller rolling straight back towards the crown. Add another nickel-sized roller on either side of this center roller.

Figure 9.55   Step 5. Set the back of the wig on nickel-sized rollers in diagonal rows that alternate direction.

Figure 9.56   Step 6. At the very bottom of the wig, use dime-sized rollers for a tighter curl at the nape of the neck. Notice how this row has two rollers on each side of center that are set rolling in towards center.

1904s Pinup Girl/Victory Rolls—The Finished Set

Figures 9.57–60 The finished 1940s Pinup Girl/Victory Rolls style set.

Once you have finished setting the wig, steam each roller thoroughly if the wig is made of synthetic hair. If the wig is human hair, soak each roller with water sprayed from a spray bottle. After steaming or wetting, place the wig in a wig dryer for 75 minutes.

To style:

Figure 9.61   Step 7. Remove all of the rollers from the wig, beginning at the nape of the neck.

Figure 9.62   Step 8. Brush through the entire wig with a large brush.

Figure 9.63   Step 9. The wig, after being entirely brushed out.

Figure 9.64   Step 10. Use the end of your teasing/smoothing brush to separate out a small section of hair in the front of the wig. Tease the underside of this section. Mist with hairspray.

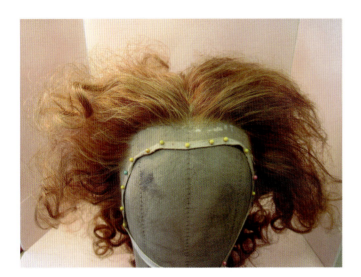

Figure 9.65 Step 11. Tease sections of hair all the way around the face.

Figure 9.66 Step 12. Gather all of the front hair on one side of the center part in your hand. Smooth it all up together with a teasing/smoothing brush.

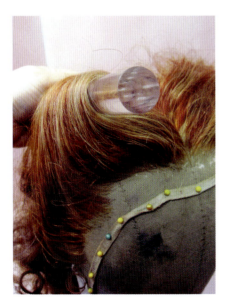

Figure 9.67 Step 13. Use a dowel rod or a plastic rod to roll up the hair into a Victory roll.

Figure 9.68 Step 14. Slide the hair off of the rod and pin it with bobby pins.

THe 1940s Pinup Girl—The Completed Hairstyle

Figures 9.69 and 9.70   Step 15. At this point, the wig is now styled in the "half up/half down" version of the Victory rolls hairstyle. The loose hair in the back has been brushed through and sprayed with hairspray to smooth the waves.

Figures 9.71 and 9.72   Step 16. You could also add a snood to the wig at this point to create more of a "Rosie the Riveter" factory worker look.

Figure 9.73 Step 17. To make Victory rolls that go all the way to the nape of the neck, begin by placing a row of interlocking bobby pins in a "V" shape under the curve of the head.

Figure 9.74 Step 18. Tease the hair below the bobby pins. You should tease the top side of the hair because that is ultimately going to be on the inside of the roll.

Figure 9.75 Step 19. Use your dowel or plastic rod to roll up another section of hair. Slide the roll off and pin it in place with bobby pins. You could also roll the hair up on hair rats and pin it in place. This is especially helpful if you want the rolls to be of an even thickness all the way down the head.

Figure 9.76 Step 20. Tuck the second roll inside the first roll.

Figure 9.77   Step 21. Use your teasing/ smoothing brush to smooth the two rolls together.

Figure 9.78   Step 22. You may need to add hairpins to ensure that two rolls are smoothly joined together.

Figures 9.79 and 9.80   Step 23. Continue rolling up sections of hair on the rod and joining them to other sections. Do this until you have created a "V" shape in the back of the wig.

1940s Victory Rolls—The Completed Style

Figures 9.81–83 The finished Pinup Girl/Victory Rolls style.

Variations

Use scarves, snoods, and flowers to add variation and style to your 1940s wigs. Another way to vary the look is to place the Victory rolls asymmetrically.

You can also create a wig with a strong wavy section in the front of the hair. This sculptural look is very typical of the 1940s.

Figure 9.85   The hairstyle in this publicity photo of Ginger Rogers has a section of sculpted waves in the front, capped off by a cluster of curls on top of the head.

Figure 9.84   This wig features both asymmetrical Victory rolls and an accent flower. This wig was styled and modeled by Thumper Gosney.

However you choose to vary your 1940s styles, be sure that the end result is sculptural and feminine.

ten

THE 1950S

{ *1950–1959* }

Figure 10.1   Illustration from *Woman's Journal* magazine, 1958 (colour litho), English School (20th century) / Private Collection / © The Advertising Archives / The Bridgeman Art Library.

1950s Women

In the 1950s, women were now leaving the factories they had been urged to work in during World War II and returning to domestic life. They were expected to look perfect for their husbands returning from the war, and they were expected to keep a perfect house without a hair coming out of place. Women usually wore their hair short and curly. Hats were very popular in the 1950s, so the hair underneath often needed to be short and neat. Fashions, such as the New Look by Christian Dior, accentuated a woman's proportions of a small head, large bust, small waist, and full hips—very much an hourglass shape.

Important Events

1950–1953	Korean War
1951	Color TV is introduced
1955	Disneyland opens
1955	Rosa Parks refuses to give up her bus seat, beginning the civil rights movement
1956	Elvis Presley appears on the Ed Sullivan show
1957	Grace Kelly marries Prince Rainier III of Monaco
1957	The Soviet Union launches Sputnik I
1959	Fidel Castro overthrows the regime of Fulgencio Batista in Cuba, establishing a communist government
1959	The airplane carrying singers Buddy Holly, Ritchie Valens, and J.P. "The Big Bopper" Richardson crashes, killing all three

Important Artists/Designers

Christian Dior, Hubert de Givenchy, Willem de Kooning, Charles James, Guy Laroche, Jackson Pollock, Mark Rothko.

Important People/Style Icons

Lucille Ball, James Dean, Sandra Dee, Audrey Hepburn, Grace Kelly, Eartha Kitt, Marilyn Monroe, Bettie Page, Babe Paley, Elvis Presley, Elizabeth Taylor.

Figure 10.2 Illustration from magazine, 1952 (colour litho), English School (20th century) / Private Collection / © The Advertising Archives / The Bridgeman Art Library. This illustration shows short hairstyles typical of the 1950s.

The poodle cut, made popular by Lucille Ball, was an especially popular hairstyle at the time.

Figure 10.3 Publicity photo of Martha Hyer for Sabrina, 1954. Hyer wears the poodle cut hairstyle.

Film director Alfred Hitchcock had a reputation for putting icy cool blondes in his films. These actresses, including Grace Kelly, Kim Novak, and Janet Leigh, became known as "Hitchcock blondes."

Bombshells such as Elizabeth Taylor and Marilyn Monroe wore more sensual, full, wavy hairstyles. Pinup queen Bettie Page made the heavy bangs that formed a slight curve on the forehead popular.

Figure 10.4　Actress Grace Kelly personifies the look of the "Hitchock blonde".

Teenage girls in this period, inspired by the film *Gidget*, began wearing their hair pulled back in a ponytail, often accented by a chiffon scarf. These girls were called "bobby soxers," so called for the short socks they often wore with penny loafers. Beatnik girls, late in the 1950s, began ironing their hair straight. Audrey Hepburn, with her short bangs accentuating her enormous eyes, helped to make the gamine look popular.

Figure 10.6　This publicity photo of Elizabeth Taylor, wears a voluptuous, side parted hairstyle, with full waves.

Figure 10.5　Audrey Hepburn, in this screen test for *Roman Holiday*, wears a gamine haircut with short bangs.

Figure 10.7　Bettie Page, pinup queen, wearing her signature rounded bangs.

1950s Men

Many men in the 1950s were still wearing the extremely short haircuts held over from military days. The flat top, a version of the crew cut that had a very square shape on top, was especially popular with young men.

Figure 10.9 Belgian singers Jacques Brel and Bobbejaan Schoepen wear pompadour hairstyles with sculpted waves in this photograph from 1955.

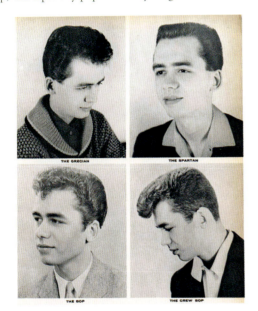

THE GRECIAN   THE SPARTAN

THE BOP   THE CREW BOP

Figure 10.8 This advertisement shows different popular men's hairstyles for the 1950s.

Non-conformist young men began growing their hair longer and styling it into elaborate pompadours. They used oils and hair grease to sculpt their hairstyles, giving them the nickname "greasers."

These hairstyles were made mainstream by performers like Elvis Presley. The backs of these hairstyles were often combed straight back on the sides with a part down the center back. This hairstyle was called the "duck tail," "duck's ass," or "D.A." hairstyle because of its resemblance to the tail feathers of a duck.

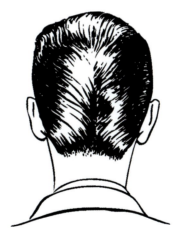

Figure 10.10 An illustration of the D.A. hairstyle.

Teddy boys in England wore fashions that mimicked those of the 1890s. Their hairstyles were often the duck tail or the quiff, a hairstyle with a lock of hair elaborately dressed over the forehead. Men's hair in the 1950s was also often wet looking, made so with the use of Brylcreem and pomade.

1950s Woman's Styling—Step by Step Instructions

This hairstyle is a combination of the deep, side parted short style in Figure 10.1 and the curlier texture seen in Figure 10.6.

Figure 10.11   Step 1. Begin with a wig that is just below chin length, with some layers. The hair should be at least 5 inches long on top—it can be shorter in the back. This style works especially well with fully ventilated lace wigs, because they are less dense than hard front wigs, making it easier to keep the style trim and close to the head. Here, I used a fully ventilated human hair lace front wig.

Figure 10.12   Step 2. Saturate the wig with water and setting lotion, and make a side part on a slight diagonal in the wig. Use nickel-sized rollers to set two rollers with some drag at the roots on the larger side of the parted hair.

Figure 10.13   Step 3. Continue setting the wig on dime-sized rollers, working down the side of the head. Include one roller that is set going down over the hairline.

Figure 10.14   Step 4. Move to the other side of the part. Use a dowel rod to form the hair into pin curls. Setting this side on pin curls instead of rollers will ensure that there is less volume on this side of the wig.

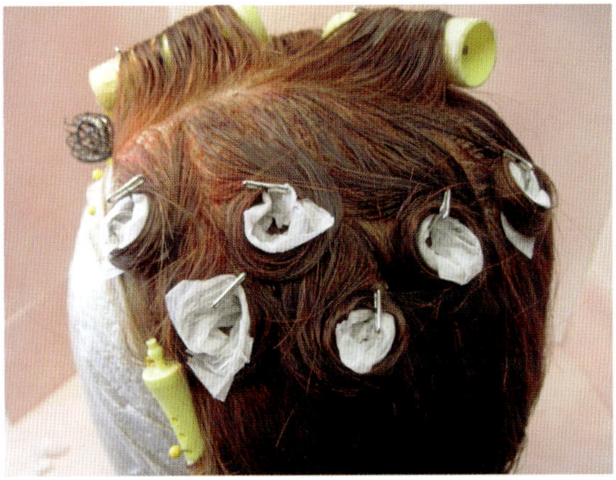

Figure 10.15 Step 5. The first row of pin curls should be set clockwise, rolling towards the face. The second row of pin curls should be set in the opposite direction, counterclockwise, rolling away from the face.

Figure 10.16 Step 6. Set three total rows of pin curls, alternating between clockwise and counterclockwise rows.

Figure 10.17 Step 7. Next, use rollers to set the rest of the wig. Begin with quarter-sized rollers on top of the head. Below the three quarter-sized rollers, drop down to nickel-sized rollers and continue setting the wig in alternating diagonal rows.

Figure 10.18 Step 8. Continue to decrease the roller size you are using as you work your way down the back of the wig. Below the row of nickel-sized rollers, set a row of dime-sized rollers, still setting in a diagonal direction. Notice how the rollers are used to fill in underneath where the pin curls have been set.

Figure 10.19 Step 9. Finish the set by setting a row of pencil-sized rollers at the nape of the wig.

1950s Woman's Hairstyle—The Finished Set

Figures 10.20–23   The finished 1950s Woman's style set.

Once you have finished setting the wig, steam each roller thoroughly if the wig is made of synthetic hair. If the wig is human hair, soak each roller with water sprayed from a spray bottle. After steaming or wetting, place the wig in a wig dryer for 75 minutes.

To style:

Figure 10.24 Step 10. Remove all of the rollers and pin curls from the wig, beginning at the nape of the neck and working your way up to the front hairline.

Figure 10.25 Step 11. Use a large brush to thoroughly brush through the entire wig.

Figure 10.26 Step 12. Next, smooth out the top section of the wig with a teasing/smoothing brush. Use the pointed end of the brush to begin pushing the waves of the wig into place.

Figure 10.27 Step 13. Use a piece of bias tape of ribbon to shape the waves in place. Pin back and forth around the head to make a continuous wave pattern.

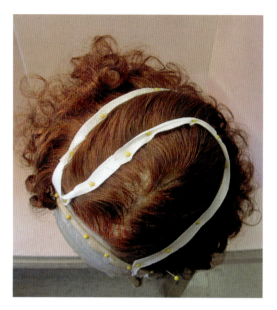

Figure 10.28   Step 14. Top view of the waves after they have been pinned in place with the ribbon. The tape should hold the waves tight to the head down to the middle of the head below the crown.

Figure 10.29   Step 15. Begin shaping the curls around the nape of the neck by brushing them up and around your finger.

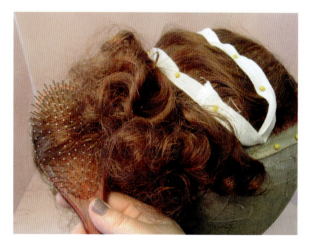

Figure 10.30   Step 16. If you wish to add some fullness to the shape of the wig, you may need to tease the lower section of curls before neatening up the locks around your finger.

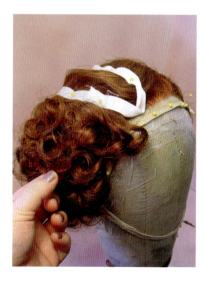

Figure 10.31   Step 17. Arrange the finished hair in a pretty way to finish off this hairstyle.

1950s Woman—The Completed Hairstyle

Figures 10.32–35 The completed 1950s Woman's style. Photography: Tim Babiak. Model: Josephine McAdam.

Variations

Part of the reason short curly hair was popular in the 1950s was its role in showing off the chic little hats that were trendy at the time. Use period hats and fascinators to create variety in your 1950s looks. Longer, more voluptuous versions of these softly curled hairstyles were also popular, especially in creating a glamorous pinup girl look.

Even longer hairstyles, such as the shoulder length hair made popular by Bettie Page can also be used during this period. Look to the pinup girl illustrations by Gil Elvgren and Alberto Vargas for style inspirations.

Some 1950s hairstyles were so short that they had few to no curls. Longer hair was often styled in elaborate updos to create the illusion of a shorter hairstyle.

Figure 10.36   Two wigs styled in longer, more voluptuous 1950s styles. Make use of both side and center parts to create variety.

eleven

THE 1960S

{ *1960–1969* }

Figure 11.1   Brigitte Bardot, 1956 (b/w photo), French Photographer (20th century) / © SZ Photo / The Bridgeman Art Library. Though this picture was taken in the late 1950s, it is representative of the teased, sprayed, tousled hair that would be popular in the 1960s.

1960s Women

The 1960s was a time of change and upheaval, not the least of which happened in the world of fashion and hairstyles. Popular styles went spinning off in a variety of directions. In the early part of the 1960s, women were still clinging to the ideal of being the perfect woman with the perfect hair. First Lady Jackie Kennedy helped set the trends with her teased bouffant style. (Aerosol cans, developed in World War II, made aerosol hairspray possible. This lighter weight styling product revolutionized the possibilities in hairstyles.) This teased hair was often girlish in shape and decoration—tall on top with a flip on the bottom (sometimes called the bubble flip), wrapped in a tall beehive, or neatly teased at the crown and accented with a headband or bow.

Important Events

1960	Female birth control pills are released in the United States
1960	Motown Record Corporation is founded
1961	Bay of Pigs Invasion
1963	President John F. Kennedy is assassinated
1964	The Beatles arrive in America, kicking off the British Invasion
1964	Mary Quant invents the miniskirt
1968	Martin Luther King, Jr. is assassinated
1969	Woodstock music festival
1969	Astronaut Neil Armstrong walks on the moon

Important Artists/Designers

Oleg Cassini, Hubert de Givenchy, Jasper Johns, Roy Lichtenstein, Emilio Pucci, Mary Quant, Vidal Sassoon, Andy Warhol.

Important People/Style Icons

Brigitte Bardot, Jane Birkin, James Dean, Audrey Hepburn, Janis Joplin, Jackie Kennedy, John Lennon, Sophia Loren, Peggy Moffitt, Diana Ross, Edie Sedgwick, Twiggy.

Figure 11.2   In this publicity photo of Elizabeth Montgomery for the television show *Bewitched*, Montgomery wears her hair in a flipped style.

As the 1960s progressed, bringing with it new attitudes about personal and sexual freedom, these hairstyles became more tousled with long, full curls. Sex symbols like Brigitte Bardot (as seen in Figure 11.1), Sophia Loren, and Ann-Margret led the way in this hair fashion.

Figure 11.3   Publicity photo of actress/singer Ann-Margret, shown with tousled, teased hair.

Falls (long hairpieces that were meant to sit on the crown of the head and match the wearer's hair color) were often used to add height and create these long hairstyles. Hairpieces were also used to create the tall elaborately arranged hairstyles of the 1960s.

Figure 11.4   A drawing of an elegantly upswept 1960s hairstyle, most likely achieved by adding a hairpiece to the wearer's own hair.

Full wigs also came back into fashion in the 1960s, thanks in part to the many girl singing groups of the era. Singers like Diana Ross and the Supremes, the Ronettes, and Patti LaBelle and the Bluebells helped to make it fashionable to wear wigs again. (It was easier to achieve teased hairstyles with wigs, plus it was much easier on the condition of one's hair!) Wigs also made it possible for these mostly African-American groups to mimic the hairstyles that were popular with white America that they would not have been able to achieve with their own hair.

In the mid-1960s, the Beatles appeared on American television and started off the British Invasion.

There was a craze for all things English and fashionable. The world was looking to fashionable Carnaby Street in London for the next trends. Hair began to move again—many girls wore their hair long with sideswept bangs. Women either ironed their hair straight, or set it on large juice cans to try and achieve the long straight look they wanted. Hairdresser Vidal Sassoon revolutionized haircutting with his famous five point cut. His idea was to cut the hair geometrically, and work with the natural movement and swing of the individual woman's hair. These short haircuts were a staple of "mod" fashion, and helped launch the careers of models Twiggy and Peggy Moffitt.

Figure 11.5   Brilliant hairdresser Vidal Sassoon cuts the hair of fashion designer Mary Quant into a short, mod style.

In the latter part of the 1960s, the hippie/flower child movement picked up steam. People protested for peace and love, and looked to an ideal of a more natural beauty.

Figure 11.6 Hyde Park Pop Festival, July 1970 (b/w photo) / London, UK / © Mirrorpix / The Bridgeman Art Library. Two flower children wear the natural hairstyle favored in the late 1960s.

Hair was often center parted, grown long, and left loose and natural in texture. These hairstyles were sometimes accented with headbands, tiny braids, beads, feathers, and flowers. African-American women also saw the rise in popularity on natural hair. After years of attempting to process their hair or wear wigs in order to conform to fashion, these women let their hair grow into Afros, a round, picked out natural hairstyle.

1960s Men

At the beginning of the 1960s, men were still wearing short, conservative haircuts. Military influence could still be seen on the still popular crew-cut or flat top.

Figure 11.7 Portrait of H.R. Haldeman, assistant to President Richard Nixon, 1971, taken by White House photographer Oliver F. Atkins. Haldeman wears a version of the classic flat top haircut.

The arrival of the Beatles and their signature "mop top" haircuts set off the trend for young men to begin growing their hair longer.

Figure 11.8 The Beatles arriving in America, waving to fans, 1964.

As the decade progressed, men's hair grew longer, eventually reaching their shoulders. Long sideburns were popular for a time; then the fashion turned to full beards. At the end of the decade, men looked very similar to women in terms of hairstyle. Men wore center parts, and long natural hair. African-American men, like African-American women, began to grow out their hair in its natural state and comb it into an Afro.

Figure 11.9 Jimi Hendrix, wearing a natural Afro hairstyle, performs for the Dutch television show *Hoepla* in 1967.

1960s Beehive Styling—Step by Step Instructions

This hairstyle was based on the styles worn by the Motown girl group The Ronettes.

Figure 11.10   Step 1. Begin with a wig that is long and mostly one length (at least 14 inches long at the nape of the neck). It is also good if the wig has a section of bangs in the front. Hard front wigs are another good choice for 1960s styles, because so many of them were actually wigs. Here, I used a lace front synthetic wig.

Figure 11.11   Step 2. Set the bang section on a quarter-sized roller, going towards the face at an angle. If your wig does not have bangs, you can set a longer section of hair in the same manner and use it to sweep across the forehead later as part of the finished style. Also note that a tiny tendril of hair has been set in front of each ear on pencil rollers.

Figure 11.12   Step 3. This version of the beehive is going to have a long curled section that comes down over one shoulder. To achieve this look, set a couple of rollers behind one ear. Use either dime- or nickel-sized rollers.

Figure 11.13   Step 4. Set several sections of hair on quarter-sized rollers, going straight back away from the face. At the side of the face, use nickel-sized rollers.

Figure 11.14   Step 5. At the crown of the head, pull a small section of hair into a loose ponytail. Begin using larger rollers (the size of a half dollar) to continue setting the hair.

Figure 11.15   Step 6. Continue working your way around the head, setting the hair on large rollers. The rollers should be set with some drag so that they all roll inwards towards the center back of the head.

1960s Beehive Hairstyle—The Finished Set

Figures 11.16–19 The finished 1960s Beehive style set.

Once you have finished setting the wig, steam each roller thoroughly if the wig is made of synthetic hair. If the wig is human hair, soak each roller with water sprayed from a spray bottle. After steaming or wetting, place the wig in a wig dryer for 75 minutes.

To style:

Figure 11.20   Step 7. Remove all of the rollers from the wig, beginning at the nape of the neck and working your way up towards the front hairline. Brush through the hair with a large hairbrush.

Figure 11.21   Step 8. Move to the crown of the head where you made the small ponytail. Use a teasing/smoothing brush to tease the hair in the ponytail. Make sure you tease the hair thoroughly so that this section is very dense. Spray the ponytail with hairspray periodically as you work to help all of the hair stick together as a unit.

Figure 11.22   Step 9. Place a hair rat in a similiar hair color behind the ponytail and pin it in place with bobby pins.

Figure 11.23   Step 10. Use the smoothing brush to smooth all of the hair around the rat, forming a cone-like shape. Pin the base of this section with hairpins to secure the hair. (Hairpins slide right into the rat, forming a firm base for the rest of the hairstyle.)

Figure 11.24   Step 11. All of the hair in the ponytail should now be formed into the cone shape.

Figure 11.25   Step 12. Separate out the long lock of hair that is going to hang down over the shoulder. Continue to leave out the bangs and the pieces of hair around the face. Pull the rest of the hair in the back of the wig into a French twist by first sweeping all of the hair to one side and pinning it up the center back with crossed bobby pins.

Figures 11.26 and 11.27   Step 13. Next gather the hair into a ponytail at the nape of the wig, twist the hair, and pull it up into a twist.

Figure 11.28   Step 14. Secure the twist with bobby pins.

Figure 11.29 Step 15. Brush through the loose ends of hair that are now at the top of the French twist.

Figure 11.30 Step 16. Use the teasing brush to tease those loose ends of hair.

Figures 11.31 and 11.32 Step 17. Smooth the loose ends of the hair around the first cone you made, making the cone bigger as you incorporate the hair.

Figure 11.33 Step 18. At this point, you should have a good sized beehive.

Figure 11.34 Step 19. Tease the hair around the face and in the bangs.

Figure 11.35 Step 20. Pull up the sections of hair at the sides of the face and incorporate them into the beehive.

Figure 11.36 Step 21. Brush the center front section of hair just behind the bangs into the beehive and use it to complete the teased cone.

Figure 11.37 Step 22. Smooth this last section of hair over and around the cone, tucking the ends in so that the beehive has a smooth, finished look.

Figure 11.38 Step 23. Top view of the finished beehive.

Figure 11.39 Step 24. Tease and smooth the bangs, smoothing them over to one side of the forehead.

Figure 11.40 Step 25. Brush the long lock of hair that is going to hang over the shoulder around two fingers in order to make the curl neat.

Figures 11.47 and 11.48   This "hippie chick" wig has been set using a combination of rollers and French braids.

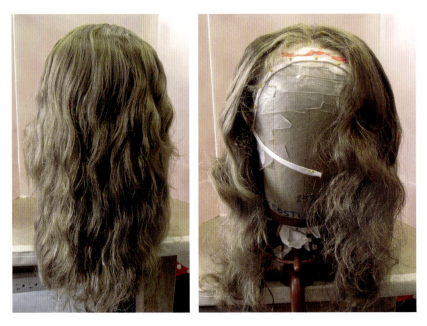

Figures 11.49 and 11.50   The finished "hippie chick" wig, after it has been brushed through.
A lace front synthetic wig was used for this style.

twelve

1970S AND 1980S TO THE PRESENT

{ *1970—Today* }

In the 2000s, fuller hair regained popularity, inspired by models like Gisele Bundchen and the Victoria's Secret Angels. The idea was for hair to have a more natural and sexy look, as though the woman had spent a day at the beach and her hair just happened to end up looking full and glamorous. Many texturizing salt sprays were created to help women achieve this look.

Figure 12.8   Candice Swanepoel at Victoria's Secret Michigan Avenue Store Hosting "The Nakeds" Launch in Chicago, IL, USA on March 31, 2010. Photo by Adam Bielawski. This model is an excellent example of the natural, sexy hair look of the 2000s/2010s.

Hip-hop music greatly influenced men's hairstyles in the 1990s. The hi-top fade (an African-American men's style that was shaved almost to the skin on the sides and allowed to grow very tall on top and then sculpted into a geometric shape) was made popular by the band Kid 'n Play. Grunge hairstyles, long unkempt hair, were worn by rock stars like Kurt Cobain. Men in the 1990s and 2000s often wore their hair in cornrows and dreadlocks. (These styles were traditionally African, but were worn by people of all races at this time.)

In the present day, contemporary hair features a lot of razor cutting (for jagged edges), and extreme hair colors. New hair dyes make it possible for hair to be any color of the rainbow. Rockabilly fashion for both men and women features hairstyles that are a throwback to the 1940s and 1950s, with women wearing their hair in Victory rolls and Bettie Page bangs, and men wearing sculpted pompadours. Hipster men of today often wear scraggly longish hair with beards. There is a strong Japanese influence in fashion as well, with anime inspired looks worn in the harajuku district of Tokyo inspiring fashion around the world.

Figure 12.9   Two Gothic Lolita girls in Harajuku, Japan.

1970s Hot Rollered Woman's Style— Step by Step Instructions

This style is inspired by Farrah Fawcett's hairstyle, seen in Figure 12.2.

Figure 12.10   Step 1. Begin with a wig that is long in the back (at least 10 inches long at the nape) with layers around the face (the layers should be 4–8 inches in length). I used a fully ventilated human hair wig.

Figure 12.11   Step 2. Part the wig in the center. Wet the hair with a combination of water and setting lotion. Use quarter-sized rollers to set curls on either side of the part. Continue setting rollers straight down the sides of the wig on either side of the face. If you are using a human hair wig, you could create this set with hot rollers, but I prefer the longer lasting set created by using water and heat to style the hair.

Figure 12.12   Step 3. Set two more rollers behind the ones on either side of the center part. These rollers have been set with drag at the roots in order to help create the "wing" shape at the front of the wig.

Figure 12.13   Step 4. Continue using quarter-sized rollers around the back of the wig, setting them horizontally at the crown of the head.

Figure 12.14   Step 5. Begin setting the back of the wig in rows going in alternating diagonal rows. The first row should be set on quarter-sized rollers.

Figure 12.15   Step 6. The rest of the wig should be set on nickel-sized rollers. Continue setting the hair in alternating diagonal rows.

1970s Woman's Hot Rollered Hairstyle—The Finished Set

Figures 12.16–19   The finished 1970s Hot Roller style set.

Once you have finished setting the wig, steam each roller thoroughly if the wig is made of synthetic hair. If the wig is human hair, soak each roller with water sprayed from a spray bottle. After steaming or wetting, place the wig in a wig dryer for 75 minutes.

To style:

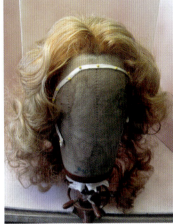

Figure 12.20 Step 7. Remove all of the rollers, beginning at the nape of the neck. Brush through the entire wig with a large hairbrush. Be sure to brush very thoroughly, making sure to get the underside of the wig as well as the top side.

Figures 12.21 and 12.22 Step 8. Once it has been brushed out, the wig should have very soft curls all over.

Figure 12.23 Step 9. Tease the hair at the front section of the wig on either side of the center part, and also at the crown of the wig.

Figure 12.24 Step 10. Use a teasing/smoothing brush to smooth the teased hair back away from the face. Use your fingers to shape the waves on top. Spray with hairspray once the waves and feathers look the way you want them to.

Figure 12.25 Step 11. Shape the curls at the bottom of the wig by brushing them around your fingers. Be careful not to overwork the bottom of the wig—it should still look soft.

1970s Hot Rollered Woman's Look—The Completed Hairstyle

Figures 12.26–29   The completed 1970s Hot Rollered Woman's style. Photography: Tim Babiak. Model: Emma Dirks.

1970s Afro Styling—Step by Step Instructions

This style was inspired by the afro looks seen in Figure 12.5.

Figure 12.30   Step 1. Begin with a wig that is layered to be about the same length all over. The longer the hair is, the larger your finished afro will be. I used a synthetic hard front wig with layers that were about 5 inches long all over the head.

Figure 12.31   Step 2. Set the front of the wig going forwards towards the face on the tiniest perm rods you can find. This will help conceal the hard front edge of the wig.

Figure 12.32   Step 3. After setting the front row of curls going towards the face, set the rest of the wig with the rollers going away from the face. If you do not have perm rods, you can also set the wig using pipe cleaners as rollers. Use an end paper and roll the hair onto the pipe cleaner just like you would roll it on a perm rod.

Figure 12.33   Step 4. Once you have rolled the pipe cleaner all the way to the roots, simply bend the ends of the pipe cleaner in towards the center. This will anchor the pipe cleaner roller in place.

Figure 12.34   Step 5. Yet another setting method you can use is to set the hair on bobby pins. This produces the tiniest possible curl, and is especially useful around the edges of the wig. I find large size bobby pins easier to use as rollers, but regular sized ones are excellent for making very tight curls. Use an end paper to hold the ends of the hair together. Slide the end paper and hair inside the bobby pin and roll it up as you would a regular roller.

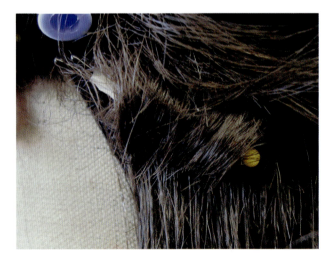

Figure 12.35   Step 5. Once you have rolled the hair to the root on the bobby pin, pin it in place with a blocking pin.

Figure 12.36   Step 6. Large bobby pins have been used to set part of the back of this wig.

1970s Afro Hairstyle—The Finished Set

Figures 12.37–40   The finished 1970s Afro style set.

Once you have finished setting the wig, steam each roller thoroughly if the wig is made of synthetic hair. If the wig is human hair, soak each roller with water sprayed from a spray bottle. After steaming or wetting, place the wig in a wig dryer for 75 minutes.

To style:

Figure 12.41 Step 7. Remove all rollers, pipe cleaners, and bobby pins from the wig, beginning at the nape of the neck. Take your time doing this—rollers this small can sometimes be tricky to unroll without tangling the hair.

Figure 12.42 Step 8. Use a wide-toothed comb to begin picking out the curls. Again, take your time and be sure that you comb through every curl.

Figure 12.43 Step 9. Comb from both the top of the curl and from the underside. This will make sure that the curls are completely fluffed out.

Figure 12.44 Step 10. Once you have the entire wig picked out, mist it with hairspray and pat the hair in place, working to create a round shape.

Figure 12.45 Step 11. Use a wire pick to create extra lift in the wig where you need it.

Figure 12.46 Step 12. You may need to trim some hairs in the wig in order to create the perfect round afro shape.

Figure 12.47 Step 13. Integrate the hair that was set going towards the face with the hair that was set going away from the face by combing through both sections with the wire pick. When the wig is the overall shape that you desire, thoroughly spray it with hairspray.

1970s Afro—The Completed Hairstyle

Figures 12.48–51   The completed 1970s Afro style. Photography: Tim Babiak. Model: Marsherrie Madkins.

1980s Permed Hair Styling—Step by Step Instructions

The reference picture for this wig was the hair on the mannequins in Figure 12.1.

Figure 12.52 Step 1. Begin with a wig that is long in the back (at least 12 inches at the nape of the neck) with bangs in the front. I used a long lace front synthetic wig with bangs.

Figure 12.53 Step 2. Set the bang section of the wig going forward towards the face on a nickel-sized roller. Small tendrils of hair have also been set in front of each ear.

Figure 12.54 Step 3. Continue using nickel-sized rollers to set the hair just behind the bangs going back away from the face. Make sure to offset the rollers so that there will not be gaps when you brush out the wig later.

Figures 12.55 and 12.56 Step 4. The rest of the wig will be set using the spiral curl setting technique. Twist each section of hair before rolling it onto a dime-sized roller. Begin with the hair at the bottom of the roller and spiral it up around the roller as you set the hair.

Figure 12.57 Step 5. Continue setting the spiral curls up over the crown of the wig.

Figure 12.58 Step 6. Set the rest of the wig in spiral curls going in alternating diagonal rows. Use pencil-sized rollers to create extra tight curls at the crown of the wig and around the nape of the wig.

1970s Permed Hairstyle—The Finished Set

Figures 12.59–62   The finished 1980s Permed Hair style set.

Once you have finished setting the wig, steam each roller thoroughly if the wig is made of synthetic hair. If the wig is human hair, soak each roller with water sprayed from a spray bottle. After steaming or wetting, place the wig in a wig dryer for 75 minutes.

To style:

Figure 12.63   Step 7. Remove all of the rollers from the wig, beginning at the nape. Be sure to carefully unwind each of the spiral curls.

Figure 12.64   Step 8. Use your fingers to gently comb through each spiral curl.

Figure 12.65   Step 9. The back of the wig, after each spiral curl has been finger combed. If there are any breaks in between the curls, use a very wide-toothed comb to blend the curls together. This should only be done at the roots of the hair—do not comb all the way down to the ends of the hair. Spray with hair spray.

Figure 12.66   Step 10. Move to the front of the wig and brush out the front section with a teasing/smoothing brush.

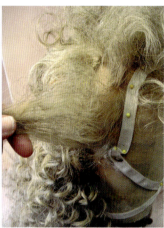

Figure 12.69 Step 12. Smooth the hair back away from the face with the brush. Again, mist the front with hairspray.

Figures 12.67 and 12.68   Step 11. Tease the front and side front sections of the wig. Mist with hairspray.

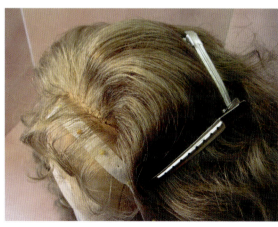

Figure 12.70   Step 13. Use your hand to push a large wave into the front of the wig.

Figure 12.71   Step 14. Hold the waves in place with duckbill clips.

Figure 12.72   Step 15. Use a wire pick to help you shape the waves on the side of the wig around the face.

Figure 12.73   Step 16. Tease the bangs of the wig.

Figure 12.74   Step 17. Smooth the teased hair forward onto the face. Use the end of your brush to push the curls into place.

Figure 12.75   Step 18. If necessary, finish off the hair in the front section by brushing the curls around your finger.

Figure 12.76   Step 19. If you want extra lift in the wig, use a wire pick to lift the hair up front the root. Spray the wig liberally with hairspray when you are done.

1980s Permed Hair—The Completed Hairstyle

Figures 12.77–80 The completed 1980s Permed Hair style. Photography: Tim Babiak. Model: Emma Dirks.

Variations

For your 1970s styles, you can create different looks by adding bangs to some of your wigs. You can also use accessories to help establish the period. For example, silk scarves were very popular in the 1970s, so you can add head wraps to change up your looks.

For your 1980s styles, once again accessories can help you create variety. Accent your wig with brightly colored scrunchies, black lace hair bows, or colorful headbands. Pull part of the wig up into a small ponytail for a half up/half down look. You could pull all of the hair into a side ponytail. Vary the texture of your 1980s wig by combing through the entire wig to create a much frizzier overall look. You can also add roots to a light colored wig using markers in a dark brown color to color in the first few inches of the hair. You can add more extreme colors to your wigs by using temporary colored hairsprays, available at many beauty supply stores.

There are many pre-made wigs available at wig stores that are great versions of 1980s and 1990s hairstyles straight out of the box. Adding accessories to the ready-made styles helps add individual character to each look. Visit cosplay supply websites for ready to wear versions of popular character hairstyles. Wigs are also becoming more widely available in a rainbow of wild colors, so it is easy to find whatever wild color combo you want without having to dye the wig yourself. Yet another way you can add bright colors to wigs is to sew in streaks of brightly colored wefting. This is especially useful when you only want sections of color in a wig, not color all over the head.

thirteen

NON-WESTERN HAIRSTYLING

Figure 13.1   Matsumoto Yonesaburo in the role of the courtesan Kewaizaka No Shosho (Shinobu) in the play 'Katakiuchi Noriai Banashi', c.1794–95 (woodblock print) (see also 236909), Sharaku, Toshusai (fl.1794–95) / Musee Guimet, Paris, France / Giraudon / The Bridgeman Art Library.

Non-Western Hair

For the purposes of this book, I have been focusing primarily on Western fashion, hair, and history. There are obviously many other cultures all over the world who also have their own unique traditions in hairstyles, dress, and culture. This could be another whole book in and of itself! Some of the hairstyles of these cultures are very elaborate; other styles are much simpler and might consist of simple braids or loose hair. Still others are much more focused on headdresses or other hair coverings, leaving the hair itself very simple. There is a wealth of research out there available to assist you in creating a global look for your characters (or for inspiring unique fictional cultures). I have chosen to discuss in detail two non-Western looks that come up often when I am working on plays and operas: the geisha hairstyle, and African tribal hairstyles.

Important Events

Geisha Styling

Geisha are traditional, female Japanese entertainers. (Interestingly, some of the first geisha were men, who entertained customers waiting to see popular courtesans.) Geisha specialize in many fine arts, including dance, calligraphy, classical music performance, poetry, and performing many traditional Japanese ceremonies. By the 1830s, geisha style began to be emulated by fashionable women throughout society. World War II brought a huge decline to the geisha arts, because many women had to go to work to rebuild their war torn country.

There are multiple stages and ranks within geisha culture. A *maiko* is an apprentice geisha and is bonded under contract to her *okiya* (geisha house). The *okiya* supplies the *maiko* with food, shelter, clothing, and other tools of the trade. Maiko hair and makeup is often what people think of when they think of the image of the geisha. Maiko wear a version of the *shimada*, a hairstyle that is similar to a chignon. This hairstyle is pulled back in the center front, sticking out wide on the sides of the face before it is pulled back and elaborately dressed in the back, depending on the age and rank of the geisha. Wax or pomade was used to give the hair a perfectly smooth appearance.

Figure 13.2 Two maiko conversing near the Golden Temple in Kyoto, Japan, photograph by Daniel Bachler. The elaborate hairstyles and special nape makeup can be clearly seen in this photograph.

Maiko also wear traditional white makeup, with two or three bare strips left at the nape of the neck, considered to be a highly erotic area (visible in Figures 13.2. and 13.3).

Figure 13.3   Woman Putting on Make-up (colour woodblock print, Utamaro, Kitagawa (1753-1806) / Musée Guimet, Paris, France / Giraudon / The Bridgeman Art Library. The back of this hairstyle is simple and shows off the back of the neck.

One hairstyle, called *momoware*, or "split peach," is only worn by maiko. Traditionally, a geisha's own hair was dressed in these styles at least once a week; modern geisha often wear wigs instead. (The tight heavy hairstyling led many geisha to develop bald spots.)

Shimada are decorated with *kanzashi*, elaborate hair combs and hairpins. These come in an enormous variety—sometimes the decorations are chosen to be appropriate to the season of the year. Others signify what house and area a geisha is from by their colors and styles.

Figure 13.4   Two geisha wearing elaborate *kanzashi* in their hairstyles.

As a geisha gains experience, she moves up in rank. Once she becomes a fully fledged geisha, her hairstyle and makeup become much more subdued (see Figure 13.5.)

Figure 13.5   A mature geisha and two maiko, serving tea at the Plum Blossom Festival, photograph by Nils R. Barth. Notice the contrast in the hairstyle and makeup of the geisha versus that of the two maiko.

Geisha Styling—Step by Step Instructions

This hairstyle is inspired by the *maiko* hairstyles seen in Figures 13.4 and 13.5.

Figure 13.6 Step 1. Begin with a long, thick, black lace front wig (at least 16 inches long at the nape of the neck). I used a wig made from synthetic hair. Unlike most other hairstyles, a geisha wig does not need to be set on rollers. You can go directly to the styling process.

Figure 13.7 Step 2. You will also need some black hair rats or pads (at least 3 inches long and 1½ inches wide) to create this style.

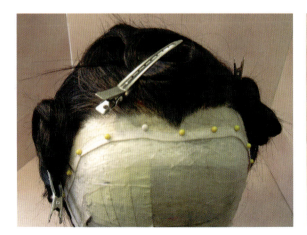

Figure 13.8 Step 3. Divide the front of the wig into three sections—the center front, and right and left sides.

Figure 13.9 Step 4. Pull a section of hair at the crown of the head into a small ponytail.

Figure 13.10   Step 5. Move to the center front section of the wig. Tease the hair at the roots.

Figure 13.11   Step 6. You may also need to use a small hair pad under this section, depending on the size and shape you wish to create in the finished style.

Figures 13.12 and 13.13   Step 7. Once you have created volume in this section, smooth the hair with your smoothing brush back towards the first ponytail you created. Add the hair to the ponytail, putting a second rubber band around the first.

Figure 13.14   Step 8. Use your wire lifting comb to add more height to this section if desired.

Figure 13.15   Step 9. Side view of the finished center front section.

Figure 13.16   Step 10. Comb the hair in one of the side sections forward onto the face. Tease the section at the roots. Place one of your larger hair pads vertically along this section and pin it in place with bobby pins.

Figure 13.17   Step 11. Pull this section of hair back over the hair pad towards the ponytail at the crown of the head, covering the hair pad completely. Use another rubber band to join this hair to the original ponytail. Spray the section with hairspray and smooth it with your teasing/smoothing brush until the hair is lying very neatly.

Figure 13.18   Step 12. Repeat this process on the other side front section. From the back, all of the hair should be joined to the original ponytail—just keep adding small rubber bands on top of the ponytail as you add in sections of hair.

Figure 13.19   Step 13. Use duckbill clips to pin the hair in the ponytail out of the way.

Figure 13.20   Step 14. You are now going to style the lower back of the wig. Comb through the back section and firmly wedge a rat tail comb into the hair. (The comb is going to serve as a tool to hold the section of hair in place.)

Figure 13.21   Step 15. Add a second comb even with the first comb on the other side of the wig.

Figure 13.22   Step 16. Pull the length of the hair up towards the crown ponytail and anchor it in place with crossed bobby pins.

Figure 13.23   Step 17. Remove the rat tail combs from the wig. Smooth the back and spray with hairspray so the hair is free from flyaway hairs. Place a second row of bobby pins a couple of inches above the first row, just underneath the base of the ponytail at the crown.

Figure 13.24   Step 18. Roll the pinned section of hair under into a small loop. You can either fold the hair or use a dowel rod to help create a uniform shape. You can also see that I placed a second rubber band in the ponytail at the crown. This wig had some long layers, so I used the second rubber band to hold all of the pieces together.

Figure 13.25   Step 19. Roll the hair in the crown ponytail around a rat. Roll all of the hair under until you reach the base of the ponytail.

Figure 13.26   Step 20. Pin the second roll you have created to the top of the wig with bobby pins. Go over the entire wig once more, spraying it with hairspray and smoothing the hairs until the wig looks perfect.

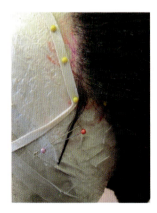

Figure 13.27   Step 21. I added a small straight piece of hair in front of each ear in order to help conceal the edge of the wig. This step is optional.

Figure 13.28   Step 22. You are now ready to decorate your wig. You can buy pre-made ornaments, or you can assemble your own. You can create your own by using artificial flowers, pre-made combs, large hairpins—there are many options.

Figure 13.29 Step 23. Many Japanese hair ornaments feature strings of dangling flowers. I created
my own ornament by taking apart an artificial flower
made up of small individual blossoms. I used a sewing
needle and heavy weight thread. I made a knot in the
base of the thread to hold the lowest blossom on.

Figure 13.30 Step 24. Next, make a knot an inch or two up on the thread,
where you want the next blossom to sit.

Figure 13.31 Step 25. Continue stringing the blossoms, making
sure to space them evenly.

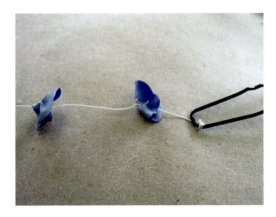

Figure 13.32 Step 26. Sew each string onto a large size wig pin.
Because I did not want the strings to slide around on the comb,
I added a small dab of latex at the base of each string to hold it in
place. Once all of the strings were in place and the latex was dry,
I added larger flower blossoms to the top of the comb by stitching
them on with thread. I also added a small drop pearl at the base of
each flower string to add weight to help the strings hang properly.

Figure 13.33 Step 27. You can create a decorative comb by winding wired flowers around the flat part of the comb. Flowers that are not on wires can be stitched in place. I have chosen flowers and colors that are appropriate to a springtime decoration.

Figure 13.34 Step 28. Tanya Olalde, craft supervisor in the Texas Performing Arts costume shop, created this *ogi-bira kanzashi* (sometimes called a rain ornament) out of found objects. She used a piece of wire coat hanger to create the base. She then added a piece of jewelry making filigree to create the fan shaped base. She then straightened brass brads and pounded them straight to make the dangling bits of metal. A hole was made in each metal piece and they were each attached to the filigree with jump rings. Finally, the entire thing was sprayed with silver spray.

Figures 13.35 and 13.36 Step 29. The ornaments have been placed in the wig. Note the place of the *ogi-bira*. A traditional red cord has been added to the front section. Painted chopsticks with a butterfly motif have been added to the back of the wig, and a small decorative butterfly has also been added.

Traditional Geisha—The Completed Hairstyle

Figures 13.37–40 The completed Geisha style. Photography: Tim Babiak. Model: Anna Fugate.

Variations

So many different looks can be created for geisha simply through variety in your ornaments. You can also vary the sculptural shapes in the back of the wig to create different looks, such as those in Figures 13.41 and 13.42.

Figures 13.41 and 13.42　These two old photographs of geisha show different treatments in the shape of the traditional hairstyle.

African Tribal Styling

Figure 13.43   Natives of Abyssinia, engraved by Aumont, c.1840 (colour litho), Dillon and Vignaud (19th century) (after) / Bibliothèque des Arts Decoratifs, Paris, France / Archives Charmet / The Bridgeman Art Library.

Because Africa is such a large and varied continent, the countries within this continent have a wildly varied look to their culture. Natural African hair texture can be manipulated into many shapes—tribal hairstyles might be made up of braids, twists, dreadlocks, cornrows, or knots. These hairstyles might be ornamented with cowries; beads; pins made of wood, bone, or ivory; medals; pieces of silver; amber balls; or metal rings. African hairstyles are often specific to status, age, ethnicity, wealth, rank, marital status, or religious beliefs. It was a common practice for the head female of the family to groom her family's hair.

Figure 13.44 Young girls from Grand-Bassam on the Ivory Coast, Emile Bayard, 1869.

their hair with red earth, red ocher, and grease; other used mud and clay in a range of colors in order to stiffen and color their hair.

Figure 13.45 A Nuba woman in Nyaro village, Kau, Nuba mountains, Sudan, photo by Rita Willaert. Notice how the ends of the braids have been dressed with mud or clay.

Hair grooming was considered an intimate and spiritual event. Hair was often groomed with black soap, shea butter, palm oil, or argan oil. Some Africans colored

African Tribal Styling—Step by Step Instructions

This hairstyle is made up of elements of several traditional African styles, which can be seen in Figures 13.43, 13.44, and 13.45.

Figure 13.46 Step 1. Begin with a wig that has at least shoulder length hair. I used a fully ventilated lace wig made out of synthetic hair. It is difficult to create this hairstyle on a wig that is not fully hand tied because the braiding techniques expose so much of the inner foundation of the wig.

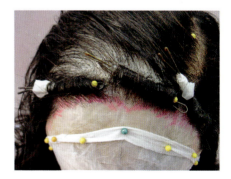

Figure 13.47 Step 2. You must thoroughly texturize the hair in the wig in order to create a successful African style. Set the hair around the hairline of the wig on large bobby pins. Use the bobby pins just as you would a roller—use an end paper to control the ends of the hair and to assist you with rolling the hair on the bobby pin (see Chapter 12 for more detailed instructions and pictures of how to use bobby pins to set hair).

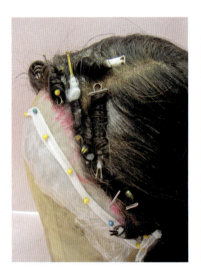

Figure 13.48   Step 3. Continue setting the hair around the face on the bobby pins.

Figure 13.49   Step 4. Set another row of hair on tiny sized perm rods.

Figure 13.50   Step 5. Behind the perm rods, you are going to add texture to the hair by creating many small braids. Secure each braid with a tiny rubber band.

Figure 13.51   Step 6. Braid all of the hair in the wig until you reach the mid-back of the head. Pin all of the braids up and out of the way with a duckbill clip.

Figure 13.52   Step 7. Set the back of the wig on small perm rods going in alternating diagonal rows.

African Tribal Hairstyle—The Finished Set

Figures 13.53–56 The finished African Tribal style set.

Once you have finished setting the wig, steam each roller and braid thoroughly if the wig is made of synthetic hair. If the wig is human hair, soak each roller with water sprayed from a spray bottle. After steaming or wetting, place the wig in a wig dryer for 75 minutes.

To style:

Figure 13.57   Step 8. Remove all of the rollers and braids from the wig, beginning at the nape of the neck and working your way up to the front hairline.

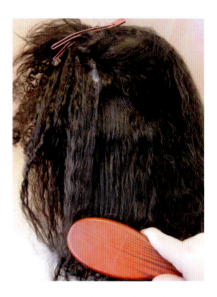

Figure 13.58   Step 9. Use a large wooden brush to gently brush through the entire wig, beginning at the nape of the neck.

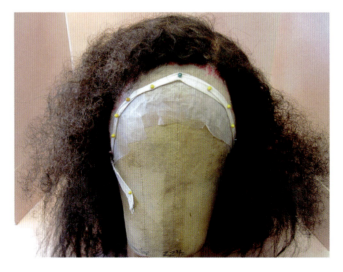

Figure 13.59   Step 10. The brushed out wig should look very soft and full.

Figure 13.60   Step 11. I dressed the front section of this wig in Zulu knots (also called *bantu* knots). Cleanly divide out a square or triangular section of hair with the end of your rat tail comb.

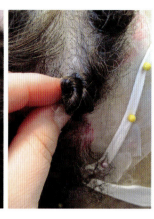

Figure 13.61   Step 12. Tightly twist the section of hair until it begins to twist back on itself. For a sleeker, neater knot, you could coat the section in hair product before you twist it.

Figures 13.62 and 13.63   Step 13. Once the hair begins to twist back on itself, continue the turning movement and wind the hair into a circular knot. (The process is not unlike putting a thread shank on a button.) Tuck the ends of the hair under the knot to secure it. You can also place a small rubber band around the base of the knot if you desire more security.

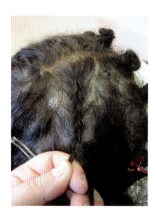

Figure 13.64   Step 14. Continue making Zulu knots all along the hair line of the wig.

Figure 13.65   Step 15. The middle crown section of this wig is going to be styled in cornrows. Because the wig I used had a built in part, I used that as the starting point for the cornrows. To make a cornrow, first separate out a long narrow section of hair. I used clips to hold the hair away from either side of the section to keep from accidentally picking up additional hair as I braid.

Figure 13.66   Step 16. Make a small reverse French braid in the section of the hair. It is very important to work very close to the scalp, picking up very tiny pieces of hair as you braid. This will help the cornrow to be very tight when you finish.

Figures 13.67 and 13.68   Step 17. Cornrow all of the hair in the wig until you reach the level of the ears in the back.

Figure 13.69   Step 18. Pin the cornrows up and out of the way with a duckbill clip. Separate the remaining hair into two horizontal sections.

Figure 13.70 Step 19. Create a larger, horizontal reverse French braid in the bottom of the wig.

Figure 13.71 Step 20. Create a second reverse French braid, braiding from the opposite side from the first braid.

Figure 13.72 Step 21. Wrap the end of each braid into a circular bun and pin in place with bobby pins.

Figure 13.73 Step 22. I chose to decorate the ends of the cornrows with beads. I used a variety of wooden beads in bright colors. Make a beading tool by forming a loop out of fine gauge wire. Finish off the end of the wire by wrapping masking tape around the end. (Be careful not to use too much tape—the beads still need to fit over it.) Place the beads on the tool. Thread the end of the braid through the loop.

Figure 13.74   Step 23. Slide the beads off the end of the wire loop onto the braid. Use the tool to gently pull the ends of the hair through the beads.

Figure 13.75   Step 24. Place a small rubber band underneath the beads on the end of each braid to keep them from sliding off.

Figure 13.76   Step 25. Once you have finished beading all of the braids, gather them into a ponytail at the back of the head.

Figure 13.77   Step 26. Create a decorative hair tie by threading more of the beads onto a strip of leather lacing. Knot off the ends. Knot the beaded cord around the base of the ponytail.

Figure 13.78   Step 27. Fold the ponytail up towards the crown of the head. Knot the leather lacing around the ponytail again so that it holds the braids up.

Figure 13.79   Step 28. Arrange the braids so that they have a natural, splayed look. You may need to use bobby pins to hold some of the braids where you want them.

African Tribal Look—The Completed Hairstyle

Figures 13.80–83   The completed African Tribal style. Photography: Tim Babiak. Model: Marsherrie Madkins.

Variations

The demonstrated hairstyle was very specifically set in order to create the finished product. You may find that you need to set your wig differently to create different looks. For highly textured looks, you might need to set the entire wig on bobby pins. You could use a wig made out of permed or textured hair; if you do so, you may be able to move right into styling without doing any kind of set. You might create a wig that consists entirely of braids or cornrows, or entirely of Zulu knots. You could also make use of different ornaments to add visual interest to your wig. Experiment with using washable clay facial masks or washable children's paint to create a mud look on the hair. (Always test this on the hair first in order to make sure they do not harm the hair in any way.)

Glossary of Hairstyling Terms

AFRO—a hairstyle, originating on people of African descent, in which naturally curly hair is allowed to grow and become bushy in a round fashion on the head.

AGGRAVATORS—short men's curls, seen in the nineteenth century, that were combed right to the outer corner of each eye.

ALEXANDRA CURL—a long spiral curl that is usually worn behind one ear.

ALLONGE—a long curly men's wig, worn during the Restoration period, that is styled in high curls above the forehead.

APOLLO KNOT—a piece made of artificial hair that is looped, coiled, and stiffened to stand up on the crown of the head as part of a popular hairstyle of the 1830s.

BAG WIG—an eighteenth-century wig where the hair in the back is contained in a fabric bag.

BANDEAU—an artificial hairpiece that was worn on the front of the head and secured at the nape of the neck with a ribbon. A bandeau could be styled in a variety of ways. It is similar to a **transformation**.

BANGS—a fringe of hair, usually brushed forward onto the forehead.

BAROQUE—a style characterized by extravagant ornament and detail.

BARREL CURL—a hollow curl that is rolled up on itself and pinned in place. This was very commonly seen on wigs in the mid to late eighteenth century.

BARRISTER'S WIG—the traditional wig worn by barristers in British courts. The wig consists of frizzy loops on top, rows of barrel curls, and two tails with tiny curls at the bottom.

BASIN OR BOWL CUT—any haircut where a bowl or basin is placed on the head and the hair is cut to the edges of the bowl. It appears in nearly all ages of history.

BEATLE CUT/MOP TOP—a hairstyle popularized in the 1960s by the Beatles. The style consisted of hair that was brushed forward onto the forehead and roughly the same length all around the head. This hairstyle was considered radical because of its length after the very short men's haircuts of the 1950s.

BEEHIVE—a 1960s' hairdo where the hair is pulled on top of the head, teased, and smoothed into a dome that resembles a beehive.

BOB—a short hairstyle for women, popularized in the 1920s, where the hair was chopped off at chin level. The bob has continued its popularity to the present day, where many different variations of the bob have been created.

BOB WIG—a seventeenth- and eighteenth-century wig with short curls at the bottom. There was both a long bob wig and a short bob wig. These wigs were most frequently worn by laborers and tradesmen.

BOUFFANT—any hairstyle that is teased around the face for volume.

BRAID—a length of hair where the strands are woven or twisted together. Three sections of hair are used to make the most common braid, but braids can be made with many more sections.

BRUTUS STYLE—a short tousled hairstyle popularized by French Revolutionaries.

BUN—any tightly wound arrangement (usually circular in shape) of hair on the back of the head.

BUZZ CUT—also called a crew cut, this is a haircut where the hair is shaved evenly around the head, at a short length very close to the scalp.

CADOGAN/CLUB—a knot of hair at the nape of the neck that was folded back onto itself and tied around the middle. This was a popular style in the late eighteenth century.

CAESAR HAIRCUT—a short layered men's haircut with short bangs that are brushed onto the face.

CAGE—a wire frame used to support large, structural hairstyles.

CASCADE—an artificial hairpiece with long falling curls.

CAULIFLOWER WIG—a short, white, curled bob wig that was worn by clergymen and physicians in the eighteenth century.

CHIGNON—a smooth twist, knot, or roll of hair, worn on the back of the head.

CHONMAGE—a traditional Japanese men's hairstyle where the top of the head is either shaved or slicked down; the rest of the hair is pulled into a small ponytail and folded up onto the crown of the head.

CLUB—see **Cadogan**.

COIF—can refer to either a close-fitting cap, or the act of creating a hairstyle.

COIL—a type of bun where the hair is wound in concentric circles and pinned.

CORNROWS—a type of braid where a narrow strip of hair is braided tightly against the scalp.

CORONET—a hairstyle that mimics a crown, usually consisting of braids wrapped around the head.

COXCOMB—a hairstyle where the hair at the center of the forehead is swept up and back into a curl. This hairstyle got its name from its resemblance to the crest of a rooster.

CRESPINE—a jeweled net for securing the hair, used in the fifteenth century.

CRIMPING—the act of pressing hair between shaped metal plates to create texture.

CYPRIOTE CURL—a sculptural curl that was piled onto a frame around the face in some Roman women's hairstyles.

DREADLOCK—a hairstyle that forms over time when naturally curly hair is allowed to wind around itself, eventually forming a solid lock of hair.

DUCKTAIL—a men's haircut, popular in the 1950s, where the hair was parted in the center back like a duck's tail. The hair on the sides was combed back and the hair in the front was intentionally disarrayed so that some pieces hung down.

FADE—a haircut, commonly worn by black men, where the hair tapers from very short to almost non-existent.

FALL—a hairpiece used to add thickness and length to the back of the head. It generally sits at the top of the head and covers to the nape of the neck.

FAVORITES—locks of curly hair that dangle at the temples.

FEATHERED HAIR—a haircut where the layers are tapered, especially around the face. This hairstyle was very popular in the 1970s.

FINGER WAVE—a method of setting wave into hair by using the fingers to mold the waves in place.

FLAT TOP—a haircut that is similar to a crew cut, except the hair is cut into a flat plane on top.

FLIP—a hairstyle where the bottom ends are curled or flipped up. A popular hairstyle in the 1960s.

FONTANGE—a women's hairstyle of the Restoration period where the hair over the forehead is dressed in wired curls. This was often topped by the Fontange headdress which was made of stiffened, pleated lace. This hairstyle is named after the Duchesse de Fontanges, who created the style after her original hairstyle fell down. She tied her hair up off her forehead with a ribbon garter, and the hairstyle caught on after Louis XIV admired it on her.

FRENCH BRAID—a method of braiding where hair is gradually added to the braid in sections, instead of braiding all of the hair together at once. This allows the braid to lie extremely close to the head.

FRENCH DOT—a tiny goatee that sits directly under the bottom lip.

FRENCH ROLL—a hairstyle where the hair is arranged in a vertical roll on the back of the head. Also called a French twist.

FRENCH TWIST—see **French roll**.

FRINGE—short hair brushed forward. Fringe is sometimes used as another word for bangs.

FRISETTE—a fringe of curled or frizzed hair worn off the forehead. Usually an artificial piece.

FRIZZLE—a short, crisp curl.

FULL BOTTOM WIG—a type of wig, popular in the eighteenth century, which was very large and elaborately curled, with a section of curls falling in front of each shoulder.

GORDIAN KNOT—an intricate, figure-of-eight knot of hair.

GRECIAN KNOT—a style where the hair at the nape of the neck was coiled and knotted to resemble the hairstyle of ancient Greek women.

HANDLEBAR MUSTACHE—a mustache style where the ends stick out past the lips and turn up at the ends. These ends are often waxed into points.

HEDGEHOG—a name for hairstyles worn by both men and women in the late eighteenth century. For men, this was a hairstyle where the hair was short all around the face and worn spiked out. For women, the hedgehog hairstyle consisted of a shorter cloud of curls around the face, with long ringlets hanging down in the back.

HIME CUT—an Asian hairstyle that consists of long straight hair with blunt bangs and a section of hair that is cut to shoulder length.

HOLLYWOOD BEARD—a short full beard where the section of hair under the lower lip and on the front of the chin area has been shaved away.

HURLUBERLU—a women's hairstyle of the late seventeenth century, where the hair is usually center parted, and worn very curly all around the head, with a few long ringlets hanging down the back. The term roughly translates from the French to "screwball," "cabbage head," or "scatter brain."

KISS CURL/SPIT CURL—a small short curl that is worn curling onto the face.

LADYKILLER—also referred to as Dundreary whiskers or Piccadilly Weepers. Long, drooping sideburns that nearly touch the shoulders.

LAPPET—a longer curl that hangs loose on the face or neck.

LIBERTY SPIKES—a hairstyle popularized by the British punk culture of the 1970s where the hair was styled into a wide pointed spike that stuck out all over the head. This hairstyle often requires the use of extreme styling products, including glue, egg whites, gelatin, starch, and hairspray, in order to keep its stiff shape.

LION WIG—the term can either refer to an eighteenth-century wig that resembles the mane of a lion, or, more commonly, a style of Kabuki wig. A lion Kabuki wig is usually white in color and consists of long bangs brushed forward onto the forehead and three long full tails of hair (one over each shoulder and one hanging down the back).

LOCK OF HORUS—a lock of hair that was left uncut over the right ear of young Egyptian boys. (The rest of the head was shaved.)

LOVELOCK—a long curl or ringlet of hair that is pulled forward to hang over the shoulder. These were worn by both men and women in the Cavalier period.

MACARONI—a male dandy or fop of the late eighteenth century. The term *macaroni* also refers to the wig style worn by these dandies where the hair in the front was dressed very tall and sometimes pointy. A small hat was often perched on this tall section of hair. The hair in the back of this wig style was usually pulled into a queue and clubbed.

MARCEL WAVE—a method of waving the hair where the hair was pressed with hot waving irons. It is a similar method of hairstyling to crimping the hair. It was invented by French hairdresser Marcel Grateau in 1872.

MOHAWK—a hairstyle where the entire head is shaved to the skin except for a strip of hair down the center that is spiked up.

MOMOWARE—a Japanese hairstyle worn by maiko (apprentice geisha). This style is known as the "divided peach."

MULLET—a hairstyle where the hair is cut short in the front and sides and left long in the back.

MUTTON CHOP—a type of sideburn that is narrow near the temple and wide at the jaw line.

ODANGO—a hairstyle, inspired by Japanese anime, where the hair is arranged in two buns on top of the head that resemble animal ears.

PAGEBOY—a long bobbed hairstyle, usually just touching the shoulders, with the ends turned under. This hairstyle first came into being as a style used on medieval boys serving under knights. It later gained popularity as a women's hairstyle in the 1930s and 40s.

PENCIL MUSTACHE—a mustache made up of a very thin line of hairs.

PERIWIG—another term for a wig from the seventeenth century, especially used by the British.

PERM—a slang term for a permanent wave. This is a process where the hair is rolled onto tiny rollers and treated with chemicals so that the hair takes on a "permanent" curl.

PERRUKE/PERRUQUE—the French word for wig.

PIGTAIL—long hair that is pulled back, cinched, and braided.

PIGTAIL WIG—a men's wig with a long queue that is bound all the way to the tip by a ribbon.

PIN CURL—a flat curl held in place by a hairpin while it is being set.

PIXIE CUT—a short women's hairstyle that has wispy layered bangs.

PLAIT—another word for braid. There are many varieties of plaits.

POMPADOUR—a hairstyle where the hair is not parted, and is brushed straight back off of the forehead with some height. Originally named for Madame de Pompadour. This term later became associated with a men's hairstyle in the 1950s where the hair above the forehead was styled extremely high and pouffed.

PONYTAIL—long hair that is pulled close to the head, cinched, and allowed to hang loose.

PSYCHE KNOT—a style where the hair is divided into two sections. The two sections are coiled and one coiled is pulled through the center of the other coil. This knot is usually placed on the back of the head just below the crown.

QUEUE—a long tail of hair, usually referring to a men's hairstyle. A queue can be curled or braided.

QUIFF—a hairstyle, similar to the pompadour, where the hair over the forehead is shaped into a sculpted curl or wave.

RAT TAIL—a small section of hair, usually at the nape of the neck, which is allowed to grow much longer than the rest of the hair.

RINGLET—any long, vertical hanging curl.

ROUNDHEAD—a name applied to the Puritans who supported Parliament against Charles I in England. The name came from their rounded bowl cuts.

SAUSAGE CURL—a long vertical curl that has an uninterrupted tube shape.

SHAG—a hairstyle where all of the hair is cut into layers of various lengths. This style was first popularized in the 1970s.

SHAITTEL/SHEITEL—the Yiddish word for the wigs worn by married Orthodox Jewish women. These wigs allow the women to follow the Jewish law requiring them to keep their hair/head covered.

SHIMADA—a Japanese women's hairstyle, usually worn by geisha.

SHINGLE—a version of the 1920s' bob haircut where the hair was cut to the occipital bone; the hair remaining underneath was cut into a V shape.

SIDEBURN—a short side whisker, worn without a beard. The style was named for the American Civil War general Ambrose Burnside.

SNOOD—an ornamental net that holds or contains part of the hair.

SPADE BEARD—a beard that is cut into a rounded or pointed blade shape.

TENDRIL—a small wisp of curly hair, usually found in front of the ear.

TIEBACK—another term for a man's eighteenth-century wig that was pulled back into a queue.

TITUS—a short layered women's hairstyle seen in the nineteenth century. This was one of the rare instances of a short women's hairstyle before the twentieth century.

TONSURE—a hairstyle seen on monks where the hair at the crown of the head is shaved.

TRANSFORMATION—an artificial hairpiece that goes all the way around the head, but does not have a crown.

UPDO—any hairstyle where all of the hair is pulled up and away from the neck.

VAN DYCK BEARD—a small pointed goatee. The style gets its name from the beards that frequently appeared in the portraits painted by Sir Anthony Van Dyck.

VICTORY ROLL—a 1940s hairstyle where the hair on the sides of the head is swept up into hollow rolls and pinned. A true victory roll has the rolls going all the way down the head until they meet in a point at the nape of the neck, forming a V for Victory.

WALRUS MUSTACHE—a large mustache that hangs over the lips and drops down at the outer corners of the mouth.

WEDGE—a haircut, popularized in the 1970s, which uses a weight line and tapered layer to create the illusion of extra fullness. This is sometimes referred to as a stacked haircut.

ZULU KNOT—an African hairstyle where the hair is divided in triangular or rectangular sections and each section is tightly twisted into a knot.

{*Appendix 2*}

Good and Useful Historical Films and Television Shows

These films can be used as a good reference for the period in question. Primary research is direct research from a historical period, and is always the most authentic reference and the one you should look to first. Primary research includes actual wigs from the period (very rare due to their rapid deterioration), portraits painted during a period, and photographs. Interpretations of other time periods, including films, are secondary research. Keep in mind—the look of a film is always visually affected by the year the film was made, so while the looks portrayed in the film may not be 100 percent authentic, they are still great for giving you a feel for the period and a place to begin brainstorming ideas and inspiring your research. There is no substitute for authentic period research, but these films make for excellent supplemental material.

Victorian

Amistad (1997)
Gangs of New York (2002)
The Young Victoria (2009)

Civil War Era/Late Victorian

A Christmas Carol (numerous versions)
An Ideal Husband (1999)
The Four Feathers (2002)

Gettysburg (1993)
Glory (1989)
Gone With the Wind (1939)
The King and I (1956)
The Piano (1993)
Topsy Turvy (1995)

Edwardian

A Room with a View (1986)
Meet Me in St. Louis (1944)
Ragtime (1981)
Wings of the Dove (1997)

Teens

All Quiet on the Western Front (1979)
Doctor Zhivago (1965)
A Night to Remember (1958)
Titanic (1997)

1920s

Cabaret (1972)
Chicago (2002)
Grand Hotel (1932)
Ninotchka (1939)
Metropolis (1927)
Some Like It Hot (1959)
Wings (1927)

1930s

Atonement (2007)
Road to Perdition (2002)
The 39 Steps (1935)
The Blue Angel (1930)
The Women (1939)

1940s

A League of Their Own (1992)
Casablanca (1942)
His Girl Friday (1940)
The Philadelphia Story (1940)

1950s

All About Eve (1950)
Funny Face (1957)
On the Waterfront (1954)
Pillow Talk (1959)
The Seven Year Itch (1955)
Where the Boys Are (1960)

Television

I Love Lucy (1951–57)
Leave It to Beaver (1957–1963)

1960s

The Apartment (1960)
Beach Blanket Bingo (1965)
The Help (2011)
Hairspray (1988 and 2007)

Television

The Avengers (1961–1969)
Gidget (1965)
Mad Men (2007–present)
The Mod Squad (1968–1973)

1970s

Annie Hall (1977)
Klute (1971)
Saturday Night Fever (1977)
Taxi Driver (1976)
Velvet Goldmine (1998)
Xanadu (1980)

Television

Charlie's Angels (1976–1981)
The Jeffersons (1975–1985)
The Mary Tyler Moore Show (1970–1977)
Three's Company (1977–1984)

1980s

Back to the Future (1985)
Girls Just Wanna Have Fun (1985)
Heathers (1988)
Pretty in Pink (1986)
The Wedding Singer (1998)
This Is Spinal Tap (1984)

Television

The Cosby Show (1984–1992)
Dynasty (1981–1989)
The Facts of Life (1979–1988)
Miami Vice (1984–1989)

1990s

American Beauty (1999)
Clueless (1995)·
Pretty Woman (1990)
Pulp Fiction (1994)
Reality Bites (1994)

Television

Beverly Hills, 90210 (1990–2000)
The Fresh Prince of Bel-Air (1990–1996)
Friends (1994–2004)
Saved by the Bell (1989–1993)

2000s

Eternal Sunshine of the Spotless Mind (2004)
The Girl with the Dragon Tattoo (2011)
Mean Girls (2004)
The Devil Wears Prada (2006)

Television

Desperate Housewives (2004–2012)
Glee (2009–present)
Gossip Girl (2007–2012)
The Hills (2006–2010)

{ *Appendix 3* }

Wig Styling Resources

This is a listing of the suppliers I use most frequently in wig-making projects. I like the products they sell and have had good luck with their service.

1 **Hairess Corporation**
   880 Industrial Blvd
   Crown Point IN 46307
   (219)662-1060
   www.hairess.com

Hairess is an excellent one-stop shopping place for wig-styling needs. It carries everything—wig steamers, canvas heads, wig clamps, Styrofoam heads, combs, brushes, scissors, pins, elastics, wig caps, wig-styling products—really, almost everything you could need. Be aware that there is a minimum order and that some items can only be purchased in bulk.

2 **Sally Beauty Supply**
   Stores nationwide
   www.sallybeauty.com

Sally's carries a broad selection of combs, brushes, styling products, styling tools, hair nets, pins, colored hairsprays, and hair dyes.

3 **De Meo Brothers**
   2 Brighton Ave
   Passaic NJ 07055
   (973) 778-8100
   www.demeobrothers.com

De Meo Brothers sells wig-making supplies primarily. This is where you can purchase wig laces, ventilating needles and holders, drawing cards, and human hair.

4 **Wilshire Wigs**
   5241 Craner Ave
   North Hollywood CA 91601
   1-800-927-0874
   www.wilshirewigs.com

Wilshire Wigs is an excellent source for all manner of wigs. It carries a huge variety of brands, and many synthetic and human hair wigs. It also offers many hairpieces (good for taking apart and making into other things), and some extension hair/wefting. I buy the Giant, Wig America, and Look of Love brands most often. Specific wigs that I find most useful are:

- the "Ashley" wig by Giant: this long, one length wig comes in a huge range of colors, including white, several different colors of gray, and bright party colors;

- the "Angela" wig by Giant: a nice shoulder-length wig, again available in a ton of colors;

- "Cassie" and "Christine" by Wig America: this is a reasonably priced long wig (Cassie is curly and Christine is straight) that comes in a nice range of colors (these come in white, but not gray);

- "Dolly" by Wig America: a great base wig to create the Hedgehog style because it has lots of long, fluffy layers;

- "Lily" by Wig America: this wig is a good wig that is shoulder length, and is good for styles like 1940s women and Cavalier men that require a medium-length wig;

- the "Fingerwave Wig" in the 1920s, 30s and 40s costume category is a nice little classic wig that comes styled and works great in a pinch.

5 **International Wig**
   Hairs to Wigs
   848 N. Rainbow Blvd, Suite 4557
   Las Vegas NV 89107
   1-800-790-5013
   www.internationalwigs.com

International Wigs has a huge selection of wigs and hairpieces. I really like their selection of weaving and braiding hair and use it frequently to both add to existing wigs and to build wigs from scratch.

6 **Wow Wigs**
   P.O. Box 3054
   Cerritos CA 90703
   1-714-228-9627
   www.wowwigs.com

Wow Wigs is another company with a huge range of wigs, hairpieces, and weaving/braiding hair.

The wigs I order most often from the Sepia brand are:

- the "Ashley" wig, which is reasonably priced and comes in a nice range of colors;

- the "Nicole" wig, which is a bit longer than the Ashley wig, and also comes in a nice range of colors, especially blondes;

- the "LA4000," which is a good quality, waist-length wig. The color range is limited, but it does come in white.

- **His and Her Hair Goods Co.**
  5525 Wilshire Blvd
  Los Angeles CA 90036

1-800-421-4417
www.hisandher.com

This is another excellent source for weaving and braiding hair. It also carries a decent selection of wig laces and nets. Its textured hair for African-Americans is particularly good.

7 **M&J Trimming**
   1008 Sixth Avenue
   (Between 37th and 38th Str)
   New York NY 10018
   www.mjtrim.com

This trimming store is a good place to buy beads, ribbons, braids, and all sorts of other decorative objects that can be used to make hair decorations.

8 **Hats by Leko**
   P.O. Box 170
   Odell OR 97044
   www.hatsupply.com

This hat supply store is a good source for millinery wire (for making wig frames), horsehair, hat bases, tiaras, ribbons, veiling/netting, and flowers (really lovely ones for hair decoration purposes).

9 **I Kick Shins**
   www.ikickshins.net

This website is a great source for all manner of funky hair things. It carries artificial dreadlocks, tubular crin for making cyberlox, strips of foam, feather extensions, and everything else you might need to make a custom anime, cosplay, or cyber look.

10 **Hair Boutique**
    (866) 469-4247
    http://mp.hairboutique.com

This website carries an absurd variety of hair accessories.

11 **Japanese Style**
    1-877-226-4387
    www.japanesestyle.com

This website has a small but nice selection of kanzashi (Japanese hair ornaments).

{ *Index* }